Learning Hypnosis - Hypnosis Application for Coaches and Therapists

Jean-Maurice Cecilia-Menzel

Published by Jean-Maurice Cecilia-Menzel, 2022.

While every precaution has been taken in the preparation of this book, the publisher assumes no responsibility for errors or omissions, or for damages resulting from the use of the information contained herein.

LEARNING HYPNOSIS - HYPNOSIS APPLICATION FOR COACHES AND THERAPISTS

First edition. October 24, 2022.

ISBN: 979-8215122969

Written by Jean-Maurice Cecilia-Menzel.

Imprint

Jean-Maurice Cecilia-Menzel

Medical practitioner for psychotherapy

Hildeboldstrasse 1, 80797, Munich

telephone: 089 44135911

e-mail: info@hypnose-muenchen-praxis.de

Competent supervisory authority:

Public Health Office Munich

Professional liability insurance with

Hiscox SA, Branch Office for Germany

Chief representative: Robert Dietrich

Arnulfstrasse 31

80636 Munich

Tel.: +49 89 54 58 01 281

Responsible tax office

Tax office Munich

Hypnosis in Mental Therapy – Table of Contents

Chapter 1: Mental and Physical Foundations of Hypnosis

Introduction to Hypnosis

Hypnosis is referred to as the state of awareness, in which an individual's attention is detached from the immediate environment and diverted to the inner experiences of an individual. Individuals undergoing hypnosis focus their attention on their inner environment. Imaginative involvement during hypnosis occurs to an extent that imaginative processes appear real, creating a hypnotic reality. Conscious awareness of the external and internal environment oscillates in daily life, however, in the state of hypnosis, the internal environment predominates. Hypnosis can be perceived as a meditative state, in which a person consciously gains access to his or her internal environment and receives verbal or visual suggestions from the therapists to yield desirable therapeutic outcomes. (Williamson, 2019)

Induction of the hypnotic state is a useful therapeutic approach to alleviate pain, anxiety, adverse effects of medications, emotional distress, and other conditions. Hypnosis has an overall relaxing effect on the hypnotherapy recipient. Hypnosis does not entirely correct an underlying pathology, rather, it is an effective approach to delivering appropriate therapy to an individual. In addition to hypnosis being conducted in a clinical setting, individuals can also be taught to undergo self-hypnosis, enabling these individuals to enter the state of hypnosis consciously and deliberately as well as use visual feedback to yield desired outcomes.

Biopsychosocial Model of Hypnosis

The biopsychosocial model of hypnosis focuses on the biological, social, and psychological factors of hypnotic responding and the interaction between these factors.

The biological aspects of the biopsychosocial model of hypnosis can be explained by measuring the electrical activity of the brain during the process of hypnotherapy. Biological factors related to hypnotic responding include structural connectivity between the right and left frontal cortices, as well as between the anterior cingulate cortex, and increased theta activity in the brain in response to hypnotherapy. High hypnotizability and stronger structural connectivity between the right and left brain regions are associated with the alleviation of pain.

The psychological factors related to hypnotic responding include hypnotizability, motivation, attitude toward hypnosis, expectancies, and proneness to fantasy or absorptive capacity. Psychological factors moderate hypnotic analgesia and hypnotic nausea relief.

The social factors related to hypnotic responding include the social context and rapport, resonance, harmony, or therapeutic alliance. Collaboration and affective bond among the therapists or clinicians and the patients are integral to hypnotic responding. Rapport is proportional to the magnitude of hypnotic response. The outcomes of rapport or therapeutic alliance are mediated by trait hypnotizability, such that positive rapport may increase the hypnotic response even when hypnotizability is low, whereas negative rapport may decrease the hypnotic response even when the hypnotizability is high.

Psychological Factors of Hypnosis

The psychological factors integral to the success of hypnotherapy include expectancies, motivation, hypnotizability, attitude towards hypnosis and proneness to fantasy or absorptive capacity. Hypnotic analgesia, types of hypnotic suggestions, and the symptoms under consideration mediate the effects of these factors on hypnotic responding.

Neurophysiological Model of Hypnosis

The neurophysiological model of hypnosis is based on the function and structure of the central nervous system, and its association with hypnotic responses. The neurophysiological models of hypnotic responses related to analgesia describe the role of hypnosis in influencing pain. The neurophysiological model of hypnosis is integral to the functioning of the frontal cortex of the brain during the process of hypnosis. In the first phase of the hypnotic procedure, the patient focuses the attention on an object during the process of induction. During this phase, the frontolimbic structures of the brain become active and engaged. This phase is described as fixation. In the second phase of the hypnotic procedure, there is dissociation or inhibition of the frontolimbic structures of the brain. During this phase, the patient becomes more responsive to the suggestions. Following this, the third phase of the hypnotic procedure corresponds to suggestions of imagery and the activation of temporoposterior regions of the right side of the brain. The hypnotic responses follow the sequence of hypnotic induction, fixation, suggestions for relaxation, and suggestions for imagery. Research also suggests that the frontal activity of the brain reduces during hypnotic responding. The reduction is further precipitated upon disruption in the functioning of the dorsolateral prefrontal cortex which is induced by persistent transcranial magnetic stimulation as well as intake of alcohol, which impairs the executive functioning of the frontal region of the brain. (Valentine et al., 2019)

Conclusion

The process of hypnosis and hypnotic responding are supported by a neurophysiological model and biopsychosocial model, which further comprises the biological, social, and psychological factors of hypnotic responding. The biological factors of hypnotic responses comprise an increase in the theta activity of the brain and the structural connectivity between the right and left regions of the brain. The social factors of hypnotic responding include rapport of therapeutic alliance and social context. The psychological factors integral to hypnotic responding are expectancies, motivation, hypnotizability, attitude towards hypnosis, and proneness to fantasy or absorptive capacity. Lastly, the neurophysiological model of hypnosis involves the structural and functional alterations in the brain in response to hypnotherapy.

Chapter 2: Theories of Mode of Action of Hypnosis

Introduction

Scientists and researchers have been working toward identifying possible mechanisms to elaborate on the phenomena associated with hypnosis. In the following sections of the article, the state and non-state theories of hypnosis are described. These theoretical models are based on knowledge related to the cognitive psychology of humans.

State Theories

The state theories of hypnosis emphasize that upon giving suggestions during the procedure of hypnotherapy, processes including dissociation or repression become activated. (Jensen et al., 2014) The state theories of hypnotic mechanisms are described as follows.

Neodissociation Theory (1974)

Hilgard's Neodissociation Theory is a classic state theory of hypnosis, proposed in 1974. The theory proposes that the hypnotic mechanisms are produced when there is dissociation with control systems at a higher level. Hypnotic induction splits the activity of the executive control system into several functioning streams. In the normal states, executive control system functions, however, does not demonstrate in the state of conscious awareness. This inability to represent itself comes from the presence of a barrier known as an amnesic barrier. Hypnotic suggestions during the process of hypnotherapy act on the dissociated aspects of the executive control system. The patient is well-aware of the results of suggestions during hypnotherapy; however, the patient remains unaware of the process responsible for the results of hypnotic suggestions. According to Hilgard, the suggestions from the therapist take away normal control from the patient. The therapists mediate the executive functions and bring about alterations in the arrangement of the substructures of the brain. In the context of hypnosis, there is a distortion of perception and memory, modification of motor controls, and the perception of hallucinations as external reality. The Neodissociation Theory is based on the experiments conducted by Hilgard, in which the hidden parts of the brain can be encouraged to stimulate true pain experiences. This phenomenon is involved in hypnotic pain relief.

Dissociated Control Theory (1994)

The dissociated control theory is based on the Norman and Shallice Model of executive control to elaborate hypnotic responding. The original version of the dissociated control theory model is based on the functional dissociation between the lower control subsystems and the higher executive control. The dissociated control theory model emphasizes the functional dissociation of the supervisory attentional system and contention scheduling system. These two systems of functioning don't work together effectively when the individuals with high hypnotizability are hypnotized. In this case, the individuals become more dependent predominantly on the automatic processes based on the contention scheduling system. This scheduling system is influenced by suggestions and contextual cues from the therapists to influence the experiences of the hypnotized individuals.

Integrated Dissociative Theory (1998)

The integrated dissociative theory is proposed by Woody and Sadler in the year 1998. The theory is based on the dissociation type and can be described as the re-integration of dissociated control theories with dissociated experience.

Integrative Cognitive Theory (1999, 2004)

The integrative cognitive theory proposed by Brown and Oakley in 1999 and 2004 is based on the nature of consciousness and the nature of perception. The ideas of this theory are derived from the response set theory and dissociated control theory. The suggested responses during the hypnotherapy are facilitated using the inhibition of high levels of attention.

Cold Control Theory (2007)

The cold control theory, proposed by Dienes and Perner in 2007, describes the difference between awareness and control in relation to the high order thought theory of Rosenthal. As per the high order thought theory, individuals are conscious of their mental states when they have thoughts about those mental states. The second-order thought can be described as thought about being present in a certain mental state. It is also possible for an individual to perceive third-order thoughts. This is possible by becoming aware of their second-order thoughts. The cold control theory emphasizes that hypnotic suggestions can yield a successful hypnotic response via the development of an intention to perform the required cognitive activity or a particular action, without the formation of high-order thoughts about the intention of performed actions.

Non-State Theories

The non-state theories of hypnotic mechanisms propose that the recipients of hypnotherapy are active doers and consider the suggestions of therapists during the process of hypnosis function as enactments. The non-state theories are based on the social-cognitive theories of hypnosis, which describe the interpretation of hypnotic suggestions provided during the process of hypnotherapy does not require effort and active planning by the hypnotherapy recipients. This results from the motivated tendencies of the hypnotherapy recipients. Effortlessness during the process of hypnosis stems from the expectation of individuals for the therapy to be effortless. The non-state theories of hypnosis are described as follows.

Role Theory (1950)

Sarbin's role theory is a non-state theory, which forms a general theoretical framework to understand the social behaviors of humans.

Socio-cognitive Theory (1986)

The socio-cognitive theory also called cognitive-behavioral perspective and social-psychological interpretation, developed by Spanos and Chaves in 1989; describes that the beliefs, expectancies, imaginings, attitudes, and attributions influence the hypnotic processes. Spanos explained the transformation of thoughts, feelings, and imaginings of an individual into their behaviors and experiences related to the role of a good hypnotherapy recipient. The construction and development of a hypnotic role are integral to the determination of response to hypnotherapy. Spanos also proposed that hypnotic behaviors are described by social-psychological processes, which are similar to the ones that elaborate on non-hypnotic behaviors of the individuals receiving the therapy.

Response Expectancy Theory (1985)

The response expectancy theory by Kirsch, proposed in the year 1985, explains that the expectancies can directly alter the subjective experiences of an individual regarding his or her internal states.

When an individual expects a certain outcome, he or she acts or behaves in a certain way in order to produce the desired outcome. Individuals engaged in hypnotic procedures have a generalized response expectancy, which influences them to follow the instructions of the therapist and produce certain behaviors, which are experienced by the individual involuntarily. The theory describes that the hypnotic involuntary responses share the same mechanisms that underlie voluntary responses. The distinctive mechanisms are associated with differences in how these responses are experienced by the therapy subjects.

Conclusion

Scientists and researchers have proposed a myriad of mechanisms underlying the phenomenon of hypnosis. The theories are further categorized as state theories and non-state theories. While state theories are associated with the actions of the hypnosis therapists, the non-state theories provide a placebo effect on the therapy recipient. The non-state theories of hypnosis are based on the social-cognitive theories and include the role theory by Sarbin in 1950, the socio-cognitive theory by Spanos and Chaves in 1986, and the response expectancy theory by Kirsch in 1985. The state theories of hypnosis include the Neodissociation theory, dissociated control theory, integrated dissociative theory, integrative cognitive theory, and cold control theory.

Chapter 3: Hypnosis – Then vs. Now

Introduction

Hypnosis is characterized by the

Hypnosis is characterized by the social interaction between the therapy subject and the therapist conducting the hypnotic procedure. During the hypnotic procedure, the therapist provides suggestions related to the imaginative experiences of the therapy recipient to alter the cognition, sensation, mood, behavior, perception, voluntary control over the actions, and memory. Hypnosis is a psychological process which facilitates the relaxation of the therapy recipient and enhances the imagery of that individual to therapeutically facilitate the recovery and overall well-being of that individual.

History of Hypnosis

The founder of modern hypnosis, Mesmer considered that animal magnetism, described as an invisible magnetic fluid present in all living beings, is the source of all the illnesses in these living beings. These illnesses can be treated by manipulation of the magnetic fluid by using his hands, the phenomenon is known as mesmerism. In France in the year 1784, the scientific commission of inquiry declared the association of the effects and outcomes of hypnosis with the imagination of an individual, although, mesmerism was demonstrated to be therapeutically effective for various health ailments. Hypnosis and hypnotic techniques were applied throughout history for various purposes, including the treatment of different health ailments. The soldiers of the World War II were subjected to hypnotic techniques, which helped alleviate the negative outcomes of the traumatic experiences of the World War II. Hypnotic techniques are also effective in alleviating the negative consequences of traumatic experiences during the childhood of an individual. In the second half of the 19th century, the term hypnotism was developed by Braid and further treatment approaches based on hypnotism were developed by Erickson. (Hammond, 2013)

Traditional or Pre-scientific Form of Hypnosis

The traditional forms of hypnosis are the most widely used forms of hypnotic procedures, owing to the conception that individuals can do hypnosis with minimum training and instructions. Traditional hypnosis is considered the easiest form of hypnosis, which depends on simple commands and suggestions by the individual conducting the procedure. This form of hypnosis uses direct suggestions and commands which may further influence the thoughts, behaviors, actions, and feelings of the individual receiving the therapy. traditional hypnosis can only be performed on people uh who are not critical or can easily follow the instructions provided by the therapist. Therefore, a therapist must assess the condition of the patient before beginning the hypnotic procedure. Traditional hypnosis also forms the foundation for stage hypnotism, which is a common form of hypnosis among comedy club attendees and party goers. Traditional hypnosis is still considered a dominant therapeutic approach that is taught in Australia and other countries. In the process of traditional hypnosis, the therapist asks the therapy recipient to close the eyes, relax completely and give up the thoughts of the external world. Traditional hypnosis can be explained further by a simple example. A treatment session of traditional hypnosis for smoking cessation comprises visualization of the negative consequences of smoking, the awful smell of tobacco smoke, and the irritation of the eyes and nose caused by the tobacco smoke. This example may give an idea to the readers about how traditional hypnosis works and can be helpful for people who were planning to stop smoking. Research studies reveal that the success rate of traditional hypnosis does not exceed 30%. However, the therapy recipients report positive outcomes. Despite patient satisfaction and positive outcomes, the relapse rates associated with traditional hypnosis are relatively higher. Moreover, the therapy recipients may not be able to yield positive effects with this form of therapy in the future. In the case of failure of traditional forms of hypnosis, the therapist may need to opt for other forms of hypnosis such as conversational hypnosis to treat the underlying condition.

Early cultures

This section describes the use of hypnotic techniques in different cultures for therapeutic purposes. The oldest cultural forms of hypnosis are sleep temples, where ailing individuals underwent proper rituals in the sleep chamber. After ingestion of herbs and the rhythmic recitation of prayers, the individuals were guided to the sleep chamber, awaiting a dream to reveal the cure to promote their healing. Similar to the idea of sleep temples in Greece and Egypt, the hypnotist states were also utilized in the practice of oracles, which comprised drinking of a herbal mixture and exposure to a receptive environment such as brightly painted images and candles to provide for a target emotional experience.

International Development of Hypnosis

Modern hypnosis was developed by an American psychologist and psychiatrist, Dr. Milton Erickson. Hence, modern hypnosis is also known as Ericksonian hypnosis. The modern approach to hypnosis is focused on understanding the need and the current environment or situation of the therapy recipient. The modern approach to hypnosis facilitates the therapy recipients to develop better cognitive skills and alter the way they understand a situation in the background of challenging circumstances. The hypnotic procedures and interventions are developed according to the requirements of the therapy recipient. The modern approach to hypnosis has relatively higher success rates as compared to the traditional approach to hypnosis. In contrast to simple commands and suggestions in the case of traditional hypnosis, modern hypnosis utilizes metaphors that enforce the creative thinking of the brain. The metaphors included in modern hypnosis can be categorized into two isomorphic and interpersonal metaphors. while isomorphic metaphors are based on a moral story, the interspersed cell metaphors are based on embedded commands, which distract a conscious mind from an unconscious one in order to process the messages given by the metaphors.

Conclusion

Hypnosis is a psychological form of therapy, which is based on the social interaction between the therapy recipient and the therapy provider also known as a hypnotist. Hypnosis is not a novel approach to the treatment of several health conditions, rather this therapeutic approach was developed in ancient times for several therapeutic purposes. Individuals from Ancient Greece and Egypt utilize the concept of sleep temples to perceive the cures to promote their healing. The traditional form of hypnosis, which is still practiced in some regions across the globe, is the simplest form of hypnosis. traditional hypnosis utilizes simple suggestions by the therapist and is useful for the treatment of different health conditions, including smoking. However, this form of hypnosis is associated with lower success rates and higher relapse rates.

Modern hypnosis is based on the current situation and the therapeutic requirements of the subject. Hypnotic procedures in the modern approach to hypnosis are developed by the therapist because of the situation and needs of the therapy recipient, therefore, this approach to hypnosis has higher success rates. This chapter provides a brief description of the transition from historical hypnotic procedures to modern hypnotic approaches.

Chapter 4: Important Terms and Phenomena in Hypnotherapy

Introduction

Hypnotic procedures are associated with peculiar terms and phenomena, the knowledge of which is essential for a more profound understanding of hypnotic procedures and the clinical applications of hypnosis. This chapter provides a brief overview of different phenomena in hypnotherapy such as suggestion, ideosensory response, ideomotor response, memory phenomena, and perception phenomena.

Suggestion

The suggestion phenomena of hypnosis also termed hypnotic suggestibility, is based on different cognitive processes sensory suggestibility, which is determined by an individual's ability to imagine the suggested, yet, non-existent sensations. Methods that promote suggestibility are known as abstract conditioning comma reflects conditioning comma use of imagination comma miss direction of attention comma and repetitive stimulation. Suggestibility is further divided into primary suggestibility, secondary suggestibility, tertiary suggestibility, and interrogative suggestibility. Primary suggestibility refers to direct suggestions provided by the therapist for either inhibition or facilitation of motor activities. Secondary suggestibility is based on the suggestions implied by the therapist for alterations in the sensations or perceptions of an individual. tertiary suggest ability is described as strangers in the attitude as a result of persuasive communications. Lastly, interrogative suggestibility refers to placebo response to hypnotic procedures. Post hypnotic sessions are provided by the therapist once the hypnotic procedures are over. The therapy recipient utilizes these post-hypnotic suggestions to deliver a response 2 hypnosis even when the process is over. The post-hypnotic suggestions become more effective in the presence of periodic reinforcement, since there is no involvement of conscious awareness of the activity. (Medknow Publications, 2011)

Ideosensory Response

Ideosensory responses and other phenomena of hypnotic procedures. Hallucination is an ideosensory response in which an individual experiences something unreal but feels that the experience is actually real. Hallucination is utilized in aversion therapy to terminate habits including nail-biting and smoking. Any of the sensory modalities can become part of the hallucination. Perception of a specific object that is not present in the environment is termed a positive hallucination and positive ideosensory response. Failure to perceive an object that is present in the environment of the stimulus is termed a negative hallucination or negative ideosensory response. Anesthesia is known as the loss or reduction in the magnitude of a sensory modality. Examples of anesthesia include insomnia, analgesia, deafness, blindness, and tactile anesthesia. Hypnotic suggestions can be used to generate pain control by an individual for different health conditions, including headaches and dystonia. Moreover, surgical interventions can be performed in the presence of hypnotic anesthesia to manage pain without the utilization of a drug. Hypnotic anesthesia can also be utilized to induce numbness in any region of the body. Hypnotic analgesia is reflected by decreased functioning of the somatosensory dorsal anterior cingulate cortex. This form of energy cannot be reversed by an opiate receptor blocker such as naloxone.

Ideomotor Response

The ideomotor hypnotic phenomenon is described as a motor mechanism of muscles that respond spontaneously to the feelings and thoughts of an individual. This is described as muscular movement as a result of an idea induced during hypnotic procedures. The therapy recipient produces muscular movements as a result of suggestions provided during hypnotic procedures. Ideomotor responses are further categorized into automatic writing and catalepsy. Catalepsy is described as involuntary immobility, rigidity, or tonicity of the muscles of the body. Catalepsy can occur when the body gets stuck in a state and does not follow the commands of the mind to produce any movements. During eyeball catalepsy, also known as the eye lock test, muscles of the body become rigid despite motor commands of movement from the higher centers of the brain. Hypnotic catalepsy is a useful procedure for the treatment or management of erectile dysfunction, insomnia, and other psychological issues associated with excessive movement during sleep. Automatic writing, including the act of doodling, is described as responding to different questions without a conscious effort of the mind, following this, the treatment recipient can then interpret the answer or the doodle which was developed during the hypnotic procedure.

Memory Phenomena

The state of the human brain during hypnotic procedures can be described as functional amnesia. Functional amnesia is a reversible dissociation of the explicit memory of an individual from the implicit memory. This is known as posthypnotic amnesia. This section will discuss different terms associated with the memory phenomena of hypnotic procedures.

Amnesia or forgetting, Is there a short-term outcome of hypnotic suggestions. Spontaneous amnesia may also represent deep states of hypnosis, also termed somnambulism. Somnambulism, also equated as sleepwalkers experience, is a phenomenon in which the hypnotized individual obeys the directions of the therapist as would an awake individual do. In posthypnotic amnesia, the therapy recipients fail to remember the experiences or the events related to the hypnotic procedure. In false memory syndrome, memories of the therapy recipient transform from the physical brain into the non-physical mind. Cryptomnesia is a phenomenon responsible for the regression of past life episodes. The information, which is invisibly stored in the brain, can be recalled in response to a stimulus provided during hypnotic procedures by the therapist. Repression can be described as vulnerability to death, shame, or hate, and profound guilt, which causes the brain to hide these events or memories so that the conscious mind becomes unaware of the vulnerability to these events. The repressed memories remain dormant for long periods of time and do not have an impact on the owner of these memories. Repression can be triggered by objects or events within the experiences of the individual. The three components of the memories, including physiological reaction, event, and emotional response, can be repressed during hypnotic procedures by the therapist. Memory recall, also termed hypermnesia, is described as the act of recalling more than the normal amount of information an individual would recall. The recalled information can be false or inaccurate, and hence, this information cannot be used as evidence in the background of court hearings. The benefits of hypermnesia include finding lost items, identifying the locations of lost items, and remembering past events. Hypnotic procedures can also be used for the management of phobias, which developed during childhood. The therapist utilizes regression, in which the therapy recipient goes back to an event in the past while being aware that the individual is not physically present in the past event. Age regression is also a phenomenon seen in hypnotic procedures, during which, the therapy recipient relives the experiences of the past, which may be related to a problem experienced in the present state. Pseudo-regression involves the identification of experiences from the past, in the form of visual cues on a television screen. Revivification is a phenomenon in which an individual relives an incident, without having current knowledge of that incident. This process requires a deeper hypnotic state and strong responsiveness to the suggestions of the therapist. Revivification can be experienced in their dreams, occurring at night. Retrogradation or dynamic regression is described as the combination of revivification and spontaneous age regression. Age progression is another phenomenon observed and hypnotic procedures, in which the therapy recipient feels future experiences in the present age.

Each progression is an important way to predict the reaction of an individual to an event occurring in the future.

Perception Phenomenon

Important terms included in the perception phenomenon include dissociation, depersonalization, time distortion, and future pacing. Dissociation can be described as the disintegration of an individual from painful regions of the body to eliminate past traumatic events associated with phobias and fears. In dissociation, the therapy recipient imagines negative events. Dissociation is an important means to decrease the emotional responses of an individual. In depersonalization, the therapy recipient acquires a new perspective and ignores his or her personal identity. In time distortion, the subjective measurement of time can be modified during hypnotic procedures. For instance, in boredom, an individual experiences an expansion of time, whereas, a person feels a contraction of time while having fun. Future pacing, also termed mental rehearsal, is a form of visualization in which the therapy recipient can prepare for success as well as identification of goals via overcoming potential hurdles.

Conclusion

Ideosensory response, ideomotor response, memory phenomena, perception phenomena, and suggestion are important phenomena associated with hypnotic procedures.

Chapter 5: Depths of Hypnosis

Introduction

The depths of hypnosis are categorized into hypnoidal, cataleptic, somnambulism, and Esdaile. These depths are arranged in a sequence of light trance to the deepest trance.

Hypnoidal

The hypnoidal depth of hypnosis also termed light trance, induces a state of relaxation. This depth of hypnosis involves the closure of the eyes during the entire hypnotic procedure. This form of hypnotic trance begins with limb catalepsy such as rigidity of the arms as suggested by the hypnotic therapist. During the hypnotic depth, there is deepening as well as slowing of respiratory movements of the therapy recipient. Moreover, the facial muscles immobilize during the hypnotic procedure, manifesting as a sunken face. Glove anesthesia may also occur in this depth of hypnosis. This creates a sensation of numbness in the hands of the therapy recipient. The therapy recipient develops a disinclination to move as well as develops a sensation of heaviness in different regions of the body during the hypnoidal depth of the hypnotic procedure.

Cataleptic

The cataleptic depth of hypnosis, also known as medium trance, is characterized by an increase in the detached feelings and complete catalepsy of the upper and lower limbs of the body of the therapy recipient. The trance state may be difficult to recognize, even though the therapy recipient feels this hypnotic state. The hypnotic subject may also develop partial amnesia during the procedure. Tactile illusions during the cataleptic depth of hypnosis may influence the subjects to experience, even though those experiences do not exist in reality. Olfactory illusions during medium trance states may influence the subjects to experience olfactory sensations, even though these olfactory experiences do not exist in reality. Similarly, gustatory illusions may influence the subjects to experience taste sensations, even though these gustatory sensations do not exist in reality. Individuals subjected to medium trance states develop hyper-acuity to conditions of the external environment of those individuals.

Somnambulism

Somnambulism is referred to as a deep trance state. In this hypnotic depth, the individuals can maintain a medium trance state even when the eyes are open. This depth of hypnosis is characterized by total anesthesia. However, the therapy recipients are capable of controlling organic functions of the body such as blood pressure and pulse rate. The therapy recipients may also experience complete amnesia, which is why these individuals may not remember the events of the hypnotic session. The therapy recipients may also experience positive or negative auditory and visual hallucinations during hypnosis. The hypnotic subjects experience sensations of floating, bloating, detached feelings, lightness, and swinging. During the therapy, the subjects may observe fading or an increase in the intensity of the voice of the hypnotist. In addition to complete amnesia, the patient may experience hypermnesia, becoming capable of recalling lost memories. The therapy subject may experience lag and rigidity in the muscular movements of the body.

Esdaile

Terms synonymous with Esdaile include hypnotic coma, stuporous trance, or plenary trance. In this depth of hypnosis, the therapy recipient is less likely to exit the state of hypnosis. Despite being aware of the auditory signals by the therapist, the subject chooses to remain in a state of trance. Esdaile is also marked by slowing of the responses of the organs, as well as inhibition of all the spontaneous activities of the body.

Variability of Heart Rate and Depths of Hypnosis

Hypnotic depth is a dynamic property of hypnotic procedures which indicates the capacity of a subject to respond to hypnotic suggestions made by the therapist. The amplitude of the high-frequency component of the heart rate of the therapy recipient is positively associated with the depth of the hypnotic procedures. Greater asymmetry of the brain activity is seen on EEG in individuals with high hypnotizability.

Conclusion

Hypnotic depth is positively associated with the amplitude of the heart rate of the therapy recipient. the four depths of hypnotic procedures include hypnoidal, cataleptic, somnambulism, and Esdaile, in the order of increasing depth of the trance state. Hypnoidal hypnosis depth corresponds to light trance, cataleptic hypnosis depth corresponds to medium trance, somnambulism corresponds to deep trance, and Esdaile corresponds to a state of hypnotic coma.

Chapter 6: Behaviors and Techniques in Hypnosis

Introduction

Hypnotists utilize different techniques to induce the state of hypnosis in the therapy recipients. Moreover, therapy recipients demonstrate different types of behavior while being in this state of trance. In this chapter, the readers will learn about the different techniques and behaviors associated with hypnosis. This chapter also provides insight regarding techniques to induce self-hypnosis.

Arm Levitation

Arm limitation is an integral technique of Ericksonian hypnosis. The process of arm levitation initiates with the therapy recipient closing his or her eyes and observing the difference between the right and left arms. The treatment recipients may report their arms being hot or cold and heavy or light. The hypnotists provide suggestions based on the sensations of each arm, as perceived by the therapy recipient. In this state of trance, the therapy recipient may believe that they have lifted their arm in their mind. The therapy recipients may also lift their arms physically in response to the suggestions made by the therapist. This represents successful hypnotic induction. (Coulton, 1966)

Relaxation Technique

The relaxation technique is among the common techniques utilized by the hypnotist. Inducing the therapy recipient into a trance state, using the relaxation technique, is beneficial to the treatment process since relaxed individuals are more likely to interact with the therapists and accept indirect suggestions. Common methods used in relaxation techniques include lying down, controlled breathing, controlled breathing, speaking in a soft tone, relaxing the body muscles, and head counting down.

Handshake Technique

A handshake is a common form of greeting in most societies across the globe. Erickson utilized the handshake technique to induce a state of hypnosis. In addition to induction of hypnosis, the therapist may also disrupt the hypnotic pattern by grabbing the wrist and pulling the subject, hence, using an abnormal handshake to terminate the state of trance. Within the state of hypnosis, the therapist can use an abnormal handshake to change the pattern of hypnosis.

Eye Cues

The direction of the eyes of the therapy recipient represents the cerebral hemisphere accessed by the therapist, during the conversation with the subject. If the eyes are looking in the right direction, this means that the therapist is accessing the conscious state of mind of the therapy recipient. On the other hand, if the eyes are looking in the left direction, this means that the therapist is accessing the subconscious state of mind. A therapist can provide a suggestion that the subject is not consciously aware if the eyes are representing a subconscious state of mind that is looking in the left direction during the therapy. In addition to this, the eyes can be fixated to a single object present in the room.

Visualization

Visualization is another useful technique used in hypnotic procedures to induce trance as well as provide suggestions. The visualization technique can be utilized for recalling positive images, positive memories, and positive experiences to modify the perception of the therapy recipient towards a negative image.

Breathing Countdown

While the breathing countdown is commonly seen in meditation, this technique is an easier way to induce self-hypnosis. During the breathing countdown, the therapy recipient is required to close his or her eyes and sit in a chair with arms on his or her lap. Followed by this, the treatment recipient breeds deeply through the nose and expires through the mouth. The person then starts the countdown from 100 by using slow and controlled breaths. Each example is counted as a single interval. At the end of the breathing countdown, the treatment recipient may be in a state of hypnosis. If one fails to induce hypnosis, the counting down shall begin with a higher number.

Body Scan

Body scan, particularly useful in self-hypnosis, initiates with an individual closing their eyes and scanning down their body from head two defeats. The person shall notice every sensation of the body such as the expansion of the rib cage with each breath, the contact between the surface of the chair and the back, the contact between the ground and the feet, the position of the finger in space, and pain in any region of the body. The process of body scan shall be conducted again, now from the bottom to the top. The technique of body scan can also be combined with a relaxation technique and countdown breathing to increase the effectiveness of hypnotic induction.

Eye Fixation

The technique of eye fixation in hypnosis can also be observed in the daily life of an individual. For instance, operation tends to zone out when looking at an interesting object in a room, despite a second person talking. If the first person is not at all aware of the conversation with the second person or does not remember ward the person said, he or she is said to be in a state of trance. A therapist may utilize the technique of eye fixation via a power pendulum or by using a swinging pocket watch to induce a state of hypnosis. These objects facilitate the access of the therapist to the subconscious mind of the therapy recipient while keeping the conscious mind of the subject occupied.

Ideomotor Response and Motor Reactions in Hypnosis

Ideomotor responses during the process of hypnotherapy are described as the muscular movements performed in response to thoughts, feelings, or ideas. The therapy recipients may also produce body movements in response to the therapist's suggestion during the hypnotic procedure. A catalepsy is a form of motor reaction observed in hypnosis. In catalepsy, the muscles of the body may develop involuntary rigidity, immobility, or tonicity. Catalepsy may also occur in the states of fight and flight, during which the body fails to follow the motor commands of the brain and get stuck in a place. Catalepsy can be utilized in the processes of induction and deepening during hypnotic procedures. Catalepsy is useful for hypnotic behavior, and the management of insomnia, erectile dysfunction, and other psychologic disorders.

Communication

Communication plays an integral role in hypnotic procedures. The characteristics of hypnotic communication include the use of figurative language as well as adopting a confident, calm, and understanding approach while interacting with the patient. The therapist shall emphasize positive changes and positive emotions, to improve the chances of healing and recovery in the therapy recipient. The therapist shall provide explicit suggestions to promote the transfer phenomena and yield desirable outcomes.

Conclusion

Communication, ideomotor responses, motor reactions, visual cues, eye fixation, body scan, visualization, arms limitation, relaxation, handshake, and breathing countdown are crucial techniques and behaviors associated with the induction and progression of hypnotic procedures. Some above-mentioned techniques can also be utilized in the process of self-hypnosis. It is important for both the hypnotists and therapy recipients to learn about these behaviors, tools, and techniques, to understand the underlying mechanisms of hypnosis and apply these tools to achieve desired outcomes.

Chapter 7: Hypnotherapy and Immune System

Introduction

hypnosis is one of the many psychological interventions, which are used to influence the immune system of the human body, and provide protection against different harmful environmental agents. The immune system protects the body against diseases, by destroying pathogens or foreign disease-causing substances. It performs this function by producing immune cells, which identify these pathogens and fight them. These immune cells are regarded as white blood cells of different types. The moon system of the human body is also associated with the human brain by the sympathetic nervous system. This means that psychological interventions can be utilized to indirectly control the organization, structure, and function of the human nervous system. The following sections of the chapter describe hypnotic interactions with the immune system of the body and the role of hypnotic techniques in modulating the function of the immune system.

Self-Hypnosis

Self-hypnosis is a useful tool, which involves the utilization of hypnotic techniques by an individual to induce hypnosis himself or herself. The methods utilized in self-hypnosis main include cognitive alertness, ego strengthening, and immune imagery. Self-hypnosis increases the activity of natural killer cells and CD8+ lymphocyte cells, which fight the virus. During stressful life events, self-hypnosis it's a useful technique to bring stability to the immune system of an individual. Individuals with high hypnotizability demonstrate significant immunomodulation which is represented by increased numbers of B cells, suppressor T cells, and helper T cells. The role of self-hypnosis in the modulation of the immune system is supported by the lateralization of the immune system to the left hemisphere of the brain. Cognitive function also has a preference for lateralization to the left hemisphere of the brain of the therapy recipient. The active component of self-hypnosis is present in the left hemisphere of the brain. This active component is associated with directed and generative imagery. These techniques trigger cognitive activation, thus, influencing the function of the immune system

Hypnotherapy and Immune System

Hypnosis utilizes different techniques, including imagery and relaxation, to alter the states of consciousness and awareness of the therapy recipient. These hypnotic techniques can be used to moderate the functions of the immune system. The outcomes may be specific to the hypnotic procedure, or may include a general relaxation response. While some studies suggest that the effects of hypnotic induction on the immune system of the human body are purely placebos, other studies suggest that this may not be true. Outcomes of hypnotherapy on the immune system of the therapy recipient depend on the hypnotizability of that particular individual. Similar to well-established treatments for strengthening and facilitating the activity of the immune system such as progressive relaxation, hypnosis also yields comparable effects. A study conducted in 1996 by Johnson et al. investigated the outcomes of hypnosis and relaxation training with reference to the immune response to phytohaemagglutinin, which is used in this study as an experimental stressor. The study revealed an increase in the responsiveness of the lymphocytes, types of white blood cells, and an increase in the levels of interleukin 1B, immediately after exposure to the experimental stressor. Hypnotizability is also associated with changes in the levels of interleukin, related to stress. Exposure to stress can mediate the release of cortisol and glucocortisol, which are tumor growth hormones. These hormones originate from the hypothalamic-pituitary-adrenal pathway. The reduction of stress during hypnotic procedures helps in mediating the pathway and suppressing the growth of tumors. Cognitive activation during the process of hypnosis, however, is associated with a short-term increase in the levels of natural killer cells. Hypnosis is also significantly associated with infections with herpes simplex virus. Hypnosis leads to upregulation of the immune response and increases the efficacy of natural killer cells against the herpes simplex virus. Cognitive activation during hypnosis influences the results of hypnosis in herpes simplex virus infection and the recurrence of the disease.

Body's Response to Stress

The students are more likely to undergo stress during the time of exams. The researchers investigated the role of self-hypnosis and hypnotic relaxation training in reducing stress during the time of exams in these students. Hypnotic relaxation training strengthens the immune defense mechanisms.

Hypnotherapy and Skin Disorders

In addition to the psychological effects of hypnosis, the immune-strengthening outcomes related to hypnotherapy are useful in the field of dermatology. Hypnotherapy alleviates discomfort resulting from pain and itching in the skin. Hypnosis also alters the patterns of dysfunctional habits, including scratching the skin. Hypnotherapy promotes the healing and recovery of several skin disorders. Hypnosis also reframes the emotional and cognitive dysfunctional patterns associated with dermatological disorders. In contrast to the topical application or pharmaceutical formulations or ingestion of systemic agents, hypnotherapy is a safe and non-invasive method to promote recovery of skin in several skin conditions, without being associated with adverse effects.

Conclusion

The immune system of the human body is related to the sympathetic nervous system. The states of stress are related to dysfunction in the hypothalamic-pituitary-adrenal pathway, manifesting as disruption in the levels of stress-related hormones, including cortisol and glucocortisol, which also function as tumor growth hormones. Hypnotherapy not only modulates the function and composition of the immune system of the human body but also influences the onset of different health conditions including cancer and dermatologic diseases. Hypnosis regulates the hypothalamic-pituitary-adrenal pathway add modulates the levels of lymphocytes including T cells, B cells, and natural killer cells. Hypnosis also alleviates discomfort, skin pain, dysfunctional habits including scratching, modulate the cognitive and emotional patterns associated with the onset of skin disorders, and promotes healing of the dermatologic conditions.

Chapter 8: Neurobiology and Neuropsychology of Hypnosis

Introduction

Hypnosis is based on the social interactions between the subject and therapist, suggestions made by the therapist, and the responses of the therapy recipient to these suggestions. Not only does hypnosis provide useful information about the psychological basis of mental disorders, but is also useful for psychotherapeutic interventions. This chapter will elaborate on the neurological mechanisms associated with hypnotic procedures, as well as the relationship of hypnosis with pathologies of the human brain.

The Neurobiological Functions Associated with Hypnosis

The neural mechanisms of hypnosis are best understood by using EEG findings during the hypnotic procedures. In early studies and experiments related to hypnosis, hypnosis and hypnotizability were found to be associated with an increase in the activity of alpha waves in the brain, as demonstrated by the EEG. Later, the researchers and scientists also found an association between imagery during hypnosis and Theta activity in the brain, as represented by EEG findings. Ray et al published a study in 1997, where he demonstrated an increase in the resting alpha activity in the temporal regions of the brain in hypnotizable individuals. Moreover, hypnotizable subjects had higher theta activity in the frontal and temporal regions of the brain. After induction of hypnosis, these individuals were reported to have lesser theta activity in the brain. In contrast to this, reduced visual activity and increased relaxation during hypnosis manifested as increased alpha activity across all the areas of the brain. The EEG findings during hypnosis also suggest that the state of hypnosis is associated with task-related activation of areas in the right and left cerebral hemispheres of the brain. Therefore, with reference to right hemisphere tasks, the hypnotizable subjects demonstrate the activation of the right hemisphere of the brain. Similarly, when these subjects are instructed to perform left hemisphere-related tasks, these subjects demonstrate the activation of the left hemisphere of the brain. (Ruzyla-Smith et al., 1995)

Suggestions provided by the therapist during hypnotic procedures stimulate activity in specific areas of the brain. In contrast to lateralization of activation of brain regions during hypnosis, it is certain that the functions of the anterior frontal lobe tend to be inhibited in response to hypnotic procedures. Owing to this association, some researchers also suggest that individuals undergoing hypnosis are similar to those who are suffering from lesions in the prefrontal cortex of the brain. Hypnosis is also associated with the activation of inhibitory processes located in the anterior frontolimbic regions of the brain.

Hypnotizability and Brain Activities

In contrast to individuals with low hypnotizability, individuals with high hypnotizability demonstrate increased functional connectivity between the dorsolateral prefrontal cortex in the left hemisphere of the brain. Moreover, in these individuals, there is increased coupling between the dorsal anterior cingulate cortex and left dorsal lateral prefrontal cortex. Hypnotic suggestions during the hypnotic procedures may reduce the activation of the dorsal anterior cingulate cortex. Pain imagined by therapy recipients during therapeutic procedures is associated with activation in the insula, parietal cortex, thalamus, left dorsolateral prefrontal cortex, and dorsal anterior cingulate cortex. Individuals with high hypnotizability demonstrate increased activity in the insula and dorsal anterior cingulate cortex during handgrip activation imagined in hypnotic procedures. Hypnotic analgesia and hypnotic inhibition are linked with reduced activity of the dorsal anterior cingulate cortex. Hypnotic analgesia may also increase the functional connectivity between prefrontal cortices, anterior insular area, and primary somatosensory area. Greater levels of functional connectivity between the left dorsal lateral prefrontal cortex and dorsal anterior cingulate cortex represent greater coordination between these two brain areas in individuals with high hypnotizability.

Association with Physiology and Pathology of Brain

In addition to the management of pain occurring after abdominal, breast, and other forms of surgeries, hypnosis is also useful for the management of anxiety and different somatic functions of the body. Hypnosis helps manage the psychological challenges in cancer patients, receiving chemotherapy, including anxiety and distress.

Conclusion

Hypnotic procedures, suggestions provided by the therapists, and responses generated by the therapy recipients are integral to the treatment and management of different psychological conditions. The activity of the brain waves in different regions of the brain are demonstrated, and the activity is recorded by the EEG. Individuals with high hypnotizability demonstrate increased levels of functional connectivity between the anterior dorsal cingulate cortex and the left dorsal lateral prefrontal cortex. The magnitude of functional connectivity and coordination between these brain areas is relatively lesser in individuals with low levels of hypnotizability.

Chapter 9: Hypnotherapy – Contraindications and Limitations

Introduction

This chapter describes the prerequisites, limitations, and contraindications in hypnotherapy. It is important for both therapy recipients and hypnotic practitioners to learn about these factors before considering and initiating the process of hypnotherapy.

Prerequisites of Hypnotherapy

Both the therapists and the therapy recipients shall consider the following prerequisites before initiating hypnotic procedures for different health conditions. It is also important to consider these prerequisites before performing self-hypnosis at home.

The therapist or hypnotic practitioner, she'll identify the individuality of the subject and consider the nature of hypnotic procedures before initiating hypnotherapy.

Before inducing this state of trance and hypnosis, the hypnotic practitioner shall listen to the requirements, needs, and queries of the therapy recipient so that the individual feels safe, understood, and respected by the hypnotic practitioner.

Hypnotic procedures and techniques are significantly dependent on the social interaction and trustful relationship between the hypnotic practitioner and the therapy recipient. While inducing the state of hypnosis, the hypnotic practitioner shall utilize specific communication skills to guide and provide instructions to the therapy recipient. Cooperative interaction between the therapist and therapy subject also involves the development and delivery of verbal are nonverbal suggestions, as a response by the therapist to the requirements and needs of the subject.

To ensure effective hypnotic procedures, the hypnotic practitioners must also accept and acknowledge the alternative reality of the therapy recipient. The words, behaviors, and attitude of the therapy recipient alter the communication and suggestions made by the hypnotic practitioner, as he or she adapts to the nature of the subject. The therapist must adapt to the words and behaviors of the subject, despite being the total opposite of his or her attitudes, words, behaviors, and beliefs. The patients should be allowed to play an active role in the process of hypnosis, to facilitate positive outcomes. In this way, the therapy recipients remain happy about their recovery and are satisfied with the interaction with the hypnotic practitioner.

Effective communication skills also play an important role in the induction, progression, and outcomes of hypnotic procedures. The hypnotic practitioners must listen, acknowledge, and integrate the concerns of the therapy recipients while performing hypnosis. This can be done by speaking the language of the patient, to increase the strength of the patient and coping abilities in the hypnotic procedures. These techniques and measures help transform the concerns of the therapy recipients into therapeutic thoughts, behaviors, and perceptions.

The utilization of hypnotic procedures during surgical interventions can be further enhanced by teaching and training the patients about self-hypnotic techniques so that the patients can become their advocates and perform an active role during the recovery process.

In order for successful induction and progression of hypnosis, the patients must focus their attention on the hypnosis as well as let go of distractions including destructive thoughts so that alterations and uncoupling of the functions of the frontal regions of the brain can take place. This also facilitates the instructions and suggestions during hypnosis to alter and govern the behavior of the therapy recipients.

Limitations of Hypnotherapy

Although hypnotic practitioners, their suggestions, and hypnotherapy play an important role in the treatment of different health conditions as well as strengthening the immune system of the human body, there are certain limitations two the applications of hypnotherapy. These limitations are listed down below.

Hypnotic tools and techniques can neither treat nor reverse genetic problems and congenital health conditions.

Hypnosis cannot prevent the onset of aging, which is an inevitable process that every individual on this planet has to undergo at some point in their lives. Prevention of aging and other such inevitable processes is beyond the scope of hypnotic procedures.

While self-hypnosis promotes self-empowerment and self-advocacy, hypnosis performed by professional hypnotic practitioners is far more effective and yields long-term positive outcomes in contrast to self-hypnosis.

The application of hypnotic tools and techniques, responses to suggestions made by the hypnotic practitioner, and the nature and magnitude of outcomes of hypnotic procedures are largely determined by the hypnotizability of the therapy recipient under consideration.

Hypnotherapy may become a costly procedure, particularly in cases where healthcare costs are not covered by insurance. Hypnotherapy also requires a trained, professional, and experienced hypnotic practitioner.

Contraindications of Hypnotherapy

Hypnotherapy is contraindicated in the following circumstances. The hypnotic practitioners and the therapy recipients must be well aware of these contraindications before performing hypnosis.

Hypnotherapy is contraindicated when a patient is suffering from significant psychological comorbidity including epilepsy, bipolar disorder, or schizophrenia.

Another important contraindication to hypnosis is that the procedure shall not be used for entertainment purposes. Hypnosis is a potent clinical tool that may have dramatic and profound effects on the physical and mental well-being of the individual undergoing hypnosis.

Hypnotherapy shall only be performed by trained hypnotic practitioners. It is inappropriate for other healthcare practitioners to perform hypnosis for their or their patient's benefits.

Conclusion

Hypnotherapy is a useful therapeutic approach for the treatment and management of different health conditions, including mental and physical disorders. Prerequisites of hypnotherapy include that the therapist must be trained, experienced, and qualified, the patient must be relaxed during hypnotic procedures, the therapist must acknowledge, accept, and consider the requirements of the subject, and shall employ communication skills that are coherent with the language, behaviors, and attitudes of the subject. While hypnosis is a safe, non-invasive, and effective therapeutic approach, it cannot be used for the treatment of genetic anomalies, and congenital conditions, and is a costly procedure. Experts discourage the use of hypnosis for entertainment purposes.

Chapter 10: Hypnotherapy Sessions

Introduction

Hypnotherapy is a potentially useful technique in different domains of the healthcare system. The outcomes of hypnotherapy are significantly associated with the willingness of the therapy recipients to reap the benefits of the hypnotic procedures and remain motivated to yield positive therapeutic outcomes. The patients can learn and become trained in self-hypnosis to acquire therapeutic self-sufficiency. Each session of hypnotherapy usually lasts for approximately 30-90 minutes and comprises different stages of hypnotherapy. Individuals with borderline psychosis and other known psychological conditions, as well as the inability to concentrate for a long duration of time, are not encouraged to undergo hypnotherapy. The following sections of this chapter describe how hypnotherapy works and the components of the sessions of hypnotherapy.

Stages of Hypnotherapy Sessions

The elements or stages of a clinical hypnotherapy session include the following.

Introduction

The introduction stage of a clinical hypnosis session comprises a detailed discussion between the hypnotic practitioner and the therapy recipient. It is rather a structured discussion with components associated with a certain objective. The patient must be specific and clear about each component of the introduction stage of hypnosis, failure to consider the components of this discussion may lead to negative consequences. During the introduction stage of the hypnotherapy session, the patient may familiarize himself or herself with the environment of the room. During this stage, the subject and the hypnotic practitioner also acquire and adapt to the necessary communication skills, which will be required in the further stages of hypnotherapy. Since certain smells can trigger certain memories, the room shall be odorless. Despite the absence of hypnosis or trance state in this stage of hypnotherapy, the hypnotic practitioner shall familiarize the patients with their experiences and the techniques utilized in the procedure. This stage is crucial to successful hypnotherapy and positive therapeutic outcomes. In the introduction stage, the hypnotic practitioner gathers all the necessary information related to the treatment, as well as obtains the case history of the subject under consideration. After fulfilling all the prerequisites and acquiring all the necessary information about the patient, hypnotherapy moves on to the next stage, induction.

Induction

The induction phase of hypnotherapy is characterized by the initiation of hypnosis. In most cases, the patient is asked to close his or her eyes and focus on physical feelings or sounds first. During the induction stage, the patients deviate their focus from the external environment to their internal environment. Based on the information gathered during the information stage of hypnotherapy, different techniques of induction are utilized. The most effective technique to induce hypnosis is to utilize a model which is already associated with the relaxation of the patient. Different forms of hypnotic inductions include visual inductions, kinesthetic inductions, and auditory inductions.

Deepening

The deepening stage of hypnotherapy is characterized by the induction of the patient into deeper and more focused relaxation states, also known as elevated states of awareness of the internal environment. The therapy recipient continues to concentrate on the physical changes of the body, including deeper breathing and dissociation from his or her immediate surroundings. The patient becomes more aware of the functions and processes in the unconscious state of mind. Structures of the brain associated with unconscious states of awareness become increasingly active during the deepening stage of hypnosis. The patient gains greater control over the unconscious thoughts and activities, which are otherwise inaccessible at the levels of the conscious state of mind. The deepening stage of hypnotherapy can be personalized according to the requirements and relaxation states of the subject. The hypnotic practitioner strives to achieve deeper states of hypnosis, however, the depth of hypnosis largely depends on the comfort level of the patient. This can be measured by the physiological parameters of the patient.

Therapeutic Suggestions

Therapeutic suggestions or post-hypnotic suggestions need to be realistic, phrased positively, achievable, and restricted to a single subject at a given time. The brain perceives suggestions more effectively when the suggestions are presented in sets of three so that the brain can select the suggestion it finds the most appropriate. The post-hypnotic suggestions are made by the hypnotic practitioner when the subjects are in the optimal hypnotic depth. The subject must be aware that they would be woken after this stage of hypnotherapy. The patient is relatively more receptive at this phase of hypnotherapy; thus, this is the ideal time when the hypnotic practitioner can make and provide suggestions related to the therapy and responses. The suggestions shall be related to the discussion during the introduction stage of the hypnotherapy. The suggestions by the therapist shall be made using the words and in the language of the therapy recipient for positive and successful therapeutic outcomes. The hypnotic practitioner may also offer ego-strengthening suggestions to promote the overall physical and emotional well-being of the therapy recipient. These suggestions are also associated with therapeutic suggestions specific to the awakening of the therapy recipient. The suggestions are based on positive scenarios in the future, as well as on the clinical and personal history of the patient. Ego-strengthening suggestions also function as therapeutic processes on their own. For instance, these suggestions may facilitate confidence-building in the subject. Ego-strengthening suggestions also aim at promoting positive thinking in the patients, which can be useful in the resolution of the problems that the patients are suffering from. Ego-strengthening suggestions serve as motivational fuel for the patients to implement the post-hypnotic suggestions and develop better coping mechanisms to manage the problems that they are experiencing. (Hasan et al., 2021)

Awakening Stage

The awakening stage of hypnosis corresponds to the complete conscious state of the patients, in which they are completely aware and alert relative to their surroundings. This stage of hypnosis is also associated with hypermnesia, which is regarded as recalling lost memories. The explicit suggestions made by the hypnotic practitioner are removed during this stage of hypnosis. The therapist may provide suggestions related to the overall well-being and general health of the subject. Counting or other signals are provided to the subject to prepare for termination of the hypnotic state.

Post-hypnosis Feedback

During the post-hypnosis stage of hypnotherapy, the patient is provided with an opportunity to ask questions related to hypnotherapy from the hypnotic practitioner, which are answered and explained by the hypnotic practitioner. During this stage of hypnotherapy, the patient might also receive feedback from the therapist, which can be applied or implemented in the future sessions. During this stage, the patient is encouraged to undergo training for self-hypnosis and practice the technique of hypnotherapy under the supervision of the hypnotic practitioner. Some therapists may ask their patients not to discuss the details of the hypnotherapy process with other individuals, during the next 24 hours. This helps the patients process the unconscious attributes of the hypnotherapy while they are sleeping. During the post-hypnosis stage of hypnotherapy, the patients are likely to forget about the events and experiences of the hypnotherapy, this is termed as amnesia.

After completion of the hypnotherapy, the patients are asked to do homework provided by the hypnotic practitioner. Homework comprises specific tasks, demonstration of certain behaviors, or specific thought processes that the patient is instructed to perform after the termination of the hypnotherapy session. In the case of the suggestion of self-hypnosis, the subject shall be instructed to reinforce self-hypnosis during the homework stage of hypnotherapy. After the termination of hypnotherapy, the hypnotic practitioner will continue to provide suggestions related to the interaction of the patient with his or her condition. Homework is a useful addition to the hypnotherapy process, as it reinforces the suggestions made by the therapist during hypnotherapy, as well as break the patterns associated with the conditions of the patient.

Future Sessions

After completion of all the six stages of a hypnotherapy session, the patient is provided with details about future hypnotherapy sessions. The time interval between the two hypnotherapy sessions is determined by the condition of the patient and the rate at which the patient responds to the suggestions made by the hypnotic practitioner. Some hypnotic practitioners may also use MP3s and CDs for the reinforcement of suggestions that they made during the hypnotherapy sessions. These tools are useful for promoting confidence, motivation, and overall well-being of the individual as well as reducing the anxiety levels and enhancing coping strategies of the therapy recipients.

Hypnotherapy Prerequisites

The prerequisites listed down below shall be considered by both the hypnotic practitioners and therapy recipients before the induction of hypnosis.

Before inducing the state of trance and hypnosis, the hypnotic practitioner shall listen to the requirements, needs, and queries of the therapy recipient so that the individual feels safe, understood, and respected by the hypnotic practitioner.

The therapist or hypnotic practitioner, she'll identify the individuality of the subject and consider the nature of hypnotic procedures before initiating hypnotherapy.

Hypnotic procedures and techniques largely depend on the social interaction and trustful relationship between the hypnotic practitioner and the therapy recipient. While inducing the state of hypnosis, the hypnotic practitioner shall utilize specific communication skills to guide and provide instructions to the therapy recipient. Cooperative interaction between the therapist and therapy subject also involves the development and delivery of verbal are nonverbal suggestions, as a response by the therapist to the requirements and needs of the subject.

For effective hypnotic procedures, the hypnotic practitioners must also accept and acknowledge the alternative reality of the therapy recipient. The words, behaviors, and attitude of the therapy recipient alter the communication and suggestions made by the hypnotic practitioner, as he or she adapts to the nature of the subject. The therapist must adapt to the words and behaviors of the subject, despite being the total opposite of his or her attitudes, words, behaviors, and beliefs. The patients should be allowed to play an active role in the process of hypnosis, to facilitate positive outcomes. In this way, the therapy recipients remain happy about their recovery and are satisfied with the interaction with the hypnotic practitioner.

Effective communication skills also play an integral role in the induction, progression, and outcomes of hypnotic procedures. The hypnotic practitioners must listen, acknowledge, and integrate the concerns of the therapy recipients while performing hypnosis. This can be done by speaking the language of the patient, to increase the strength of the patient and coping abilities in the hypnotic procedures. These techniques and measures help transform the concerns of the therapy recipients into therapeutic thoughts, behaviors, and perceptions.

The utilization of hypnotic procedures during surgical interventions can be further enhanced by teaching and training the patients about self-hypnotic techniques so that the patients can become their advocates and perform an active role during the recovery process.

For successful induction and progression of hypnosis, the patients must focus their attention on the hypnosis as well as let go of distractions including destructive thoughts so that alterations and uncoupling of the functions of the frontal regions of the brain can take place. This also facilitates the instructions and suggestions during hypnosis to alter and govern the behavior of the therapy recipients.

Patient Education

Before the initiation of hypnotherapy, the patients must be provided with adequate knowledge of the hypnotic techniques used during the process, attributes of their surroundings, duration of the session, experiences during the hypnotherapy, and possible outcomes of these hypnotic procedures. Patient education and compliance facilitate the relaxed state of the patient during the process of hypnosis, as well as improves the outcomes of hypnotherapy.

Conclusion

This chapter describes the six stages of a clinical hypnotherapy sessions, which included introduction, induction, deepening, post-hypnotic suggestions or therapeutic suggestions, awakening stage, and post-hypnosis feedback. Each stage is crucial to the process of hypnotherapy and influences the outcomes and success of the hypnotic procedures. This section also elaborates on the prerequisites for hypnotherapy and describes the use of MP3s and CDs by hypnotic practitioners to further ensure the reinforcement of suggestions made during the process of hypnotherapy. Lastly, the chapter sheds light on the importance and measures to promote patient education about the mechanisms of hypnotherapy.

Chapter 11: Self-Hypnosis

Overview of Self-Hypnosis

Some hypnosis theories suggest that all forms of hypnosis are self-hypnosis, which may hold true to some extent, since individuals undergoing hypnotic procedures cannot be held against their will during the process. Therefore, compliance and agreement to the hypnotic procedures is an important element of hypnotherapy. The state of self-hypnosis involves the induction of an individual to a focused state, utilizing their awareness as the operator for the hypnotic process. The individuals may also offer suggestions, which may influence their unconscious processes or allow them to gain access to these processes and events. In contrast to hypnosis performed by a professional and trained hypnotic practitioner, self-hypnosis tends to be less intense and the individuals undergoing this process report difficulties while achieving relaxation at the start of hypnosis. However, self-hypnosis has several advantages over hypnotherapy offered by hypnotic practitioners. The advantages may include increased perception of control over experiences during hypnosis and increased ability to experience the overall hypnotic procedure. Self-hypnosis can be best taught while an individual is in a state of hypnosis. An individual learns the process of self-hypnosis both on a physical level and cognitive level. This ensures that the individuals are capable of repeating the process and experiencing the event according to the description that they are provided of that event. This chapter highlights the benefits of learning self-hypnosis and how individuals can prepare themselves for self-hypnosis.

Benefits of Self-Hypnosis

Following the benefits of learning and implementing self-hypnosis.

Self-hypnosis is a useful tool for stress management. In a stress-inducing event, the autonomic nervous system of the body becomes activated. The autonomic nervous system further comprises sympathetic and parasympathetic nervous systems. The sympathetic domain of the autonomic nervous system is responsible for the production of physiological and biochemical alterations to prepare an individual to produce a certain response to the stressor. Followed by this, the parasympathetic nervous system of the body restores the physiological and biochemical functions of the body, giving rise to a circuit, regarded as the stress cycle. Self-hypnosis strengthens the functioning of the parasympathetic nervous system to induce a relaxed state. Self-hypnosis enables the individual to safely complete their stress cycle and respond more effectively to the stressors.

Self-hypnosis is a useful distraction technique, which is an integral part of the naturally occurring processes. Self-hypnosis provides a state of absorption in which the individuals detach themselves from their immediate surroundings and indulge themselves in the internal environment. Self-hypnosis is relatively more accessible, and the individuals undergoing this process can effectively alter the perception of surrounding events. Alteration of sensory experiences is particularly useful for patients who are subjected to surgical interventions or suffering from physical pain. Self-hypnosis helps these individuals detach from their immediate surroundings and shift their focus. This produces alterations in the perception of pain and can even transform pain into another form of sensory experience.

Self-hypnosis is also used as a personal enhancement tool by individuals to shift their attention to positive events in life. Individuals with relatively low self-esteem focus on the negative attributes of a presenting event, condition, or experience. These individuals are encouraged to utilize self-hypnosis to perceive positive aspects of the given conditions, experiences, or events.

Patients may perceive a lack of control during the intake of medications or while undergoing medical procedures. Self-hypnosis is a useful strategy for encouraging a perceived sense of control in these individuals. This strategy is particularly for patients who are suffering from chronic health conditions.

Preparations for Self-Hypnosis

Certain preparatory measures must be undertaken before initiating the process of self-hypnosis. These preparatory measures are listed as follows.

An individual must set a duration for self-hypnosis before initiating the process. The optimum duration of self-hypnosis is 20 minutes. Instead of setting an external alarm, an individual must set the time internally, which increases the trust of the patient related to his or her ability to control the internal states. Accuracy of the perception of time duration is a useful measure of the healthy functioning of the individual. Waking before the set time indicates stress, whereas, waking after the set duration indicates lethargy or lack of motivation. Individuals undergoing self-hypnosis may refer to their heart rate to calculate the time. Therefore, a faster heartbeat during times of stress may cause the patient to perceive a faster duration of self-hypnosis. The patients are encouraged to practice self-hypnosis right after waking up and right before going to sleep. This prepares the individuals for the day ahead in the morning as well as helps these individuals let go of worries and stress before sleeping.

An individual may choose a specific location and time, where they remain undisturbed throughout the process and their attention remains focused on the therapy process.

When performed in the morning, individuals are encouraged to sit in a reclined chair. However, for self-hypnosis practiced during the night, before sleeping, the patients are encouraged to lie down in a prone position, as this position is associated with rest and sleep.

The patients are also required to attain a neutral posture before initiating the process of self-hypnosis. The neutral posture comprises the placement of arms on the lap or by the side, and the feet shall remain uncrossed. Neutral posture during self-hypnosis ensures that there are no distractions due to paresthesia of the limbs. Crossed arms or legs and other postures are associated with stress, tension, and sleep.

An individual is also required to close his or her eyes before the beginning of the process of self-hypnosis. Closure of the eyes increases the internal awareness of an individual.

In the case of self-hypnosis, similar stages are observed as in clinical hypnotherapy – induction, deepening, therapeutic suggestions, ego strengthening, and awakening.

Conclusion

Self-hypnosis is a useful tool utilized by the patients themselves for the treatment and management of different health conditions, as well as enhancing the overall well-being of an individual. The chapter describes the benefits, preparatory measures, and the steps involved in self-hypnosis.

Chapter 12: Hypnosis for Weight Loss

Introduction

Bay City is described as a chronic metabolic disorder, caused by an imbalance between the expenditure of energy and the intake of energy each day. In individuals with obesity, the body fat mass is relatively higher than the amount of lean body mass. Obesity deteriorates the quality of life of affected individuals add is a modifiable, and preventable cause of death. Short-term management of obesity comprises the provision of protective care to the affected individuals. The prevention and management of obesity over long periods of time also play an important role in reducing the global burden of obesity. Common treatment approaches utilized for the treatment of obesity and weight loss behavioral changes, dietary modifications, increased physical activity, pharmacological therapy, and surgical interventions. Adipokines including adiponectin and leptin are significantly associated with the onset of obesity, energy homeostasis, neuroendocrine function, and regulation of the metabolism of the body. Recently, hypnotherapy and chemical hypnosis have been adapted to facilitate the treatment of different health conditions, including medical and psychological ailments. Studies have also demonstrated the role of hypnosis in promoting weight loss in individuals suffering from obesity.

Hypnotherapy Sessions for Weight Loss

This section describes the first and second hypnosis sessions to mediate weight loss. In the first stage of hypnotherapy for mediating weight loss, therapeutic cooperation between the hypnotic therapist and the patient is established via preliminary talks. During this stage of hypnotherapy, the patient is educated about the techniques used in hypnosis, the expectations of the patient, and whether the patient qualifies for hypnosis. The nutritional habits are also assessed during this stage of hypnotherapy. The second stage of hypnotherapy involves the development of a hypnotic structure of the mind via the processes of convincing, deepening, preparing, and induction. Convincing involves the preparation of an individual to focus attention on the suggestions and respond to the suggestions made by the therapist during hypnosis. Induction refers to processes that are involved in the development of the state of hypnosis. Ego strengthening techniques of hypnosis are applied during the initiation and termination of deepening. Between the hypnotic sessions, the hypnotic practitioner provides suggestions to the subjects regarding the consumption of a balanced and healthy diet, as well as regarding the nutritional habits of the individual. After these two stages of hypnotherapy, the hypnotic session is terminated by providing wake-up suggestions to the subject.

Mechanisms of Hypnotherapy and Weight Loss

Following the hypnotherapy sessions, the body mass index BMI scores of the subjects tend to decrease significantly. Relaxation techniques employed during hypnosis as well as suggestions provided by hypnotic practitioners during hypnotherapy are useful for modifying the eating habits of obese individuals. As compared to serum levels of leptin, measured before hypnotherapy sessions, the leptin levels decrease after the subjects receive hypnotherapy. The decline in the levels of leptin is associated with concurrent weight loss in the therapy recipients. Moreover, the levels of adiponectin in the serum of obese individuals tend to increase after these individuals receive hypnotherapy for weight loss. The rise in the levels of serum adiponectin is associated with a decrease in insulin resistance, which in turn is associated with weight loss. Studies suggest that BMI scores of obese individuals are positively associated with the levels of adipokines in the serum of these individuals. The levels of adipokines including leptin differ in serum measurements conducted before and after the hypnotherapy sessions. The measured leptin levels correlate with the BMI scores, measured before and after the hypnotherapy sessions.

Conclusion

Weight loss is an important strategy for obese individuals, in order to improve their quality of life as well as reduce dependence on pharmaceutical formulations. In addition to dietary modifications, lifestyle changes, and medications, hypnotherapy sessions are useful for mediating weight loss in obese individuals. In the case of obesity, the levels of leptin in this serum are increased, whereas the levels of adiponectin are relatively decreased in the serum of individuals suffering from obesity. Hypnotherapy sessions tend to reduce the levels of leptin while increasing the levels of adiponectin in the serum of obese individuals, as recorded after the termination of hypnotherapy sessions. Hypnotherapy sessions are also associated with lowering the BMI scores in obese individuals.

Chapter 13: Hypnosis for Anxiety

Introduction

The majority of the methods utilized in hypnotherapy sessions include suggestions for relaxation, however, the most important component of hypnotherapy sessions is induction of the state of focused concentration and attention of the therapy recipient. Hypnotic responsiveness can be described as the response of an individual to the suggestions made by the hypnotic therapist. Only a small proportion of the total number of individuals who receive hypnotherapy are unresponsive to hypnosis. In the cases of hypnotherapy for achieving relief from anxiety, the majority of the therapy recipients are sufficiently responsive to the therapy. Both self-hypnosis and hypnosis performed by the hypnotic practitioner are useful for the treatment of anxiety and other anxiety-related disorders. Anxiety may also be associated with cancers, burns, oral surgery, dental procedures, and surgical interventions.

Hypnotherapy and Anxiety

A combination of hypnosis and cognitive-behavioral therapy leads to successful and positive therapeutic outcomes for anxiety. The addition of hypnosis to the treatment regimen may increase the efficacy of cognitive-behavioral therapy and yield desirable outcomes. When performed alone, cognitive behavioral therapy is less efficacious as compared to the administration of cognitive-behavioral therapy with hypnosis. Self-hypnosis training is comparable to cognitive-behavioral therapy for achieving muscle relaxation and reducing anxiety. The outcomes of hypnosis and cognitive behavioral therapy for the treatment of anxiety, also depend on the response of individuals to these treatments, as well as the hypnotizability of these individuals. Individuals practicing self-hypnosis for the treatment and management of anxiety, are more likely to achieve greater cognitive changes and perceive greater efficacy of the treatment. Autogenic training is a useful form of self-hypnosis, which mediates the functioning of the autonomic nervous system. Individuals undergoing autogenic training tend to reduce sympathetic tone and improve the activity of the parasympathetic nervous system, after a hypnotherapy session. Autogenic training leads to significant reductions in systolic blood pressure, diastolic blood pressure, pulse rate, and state and trait anxiety. (Hypnotherapy for Aniety - Google Search, 2020)

In addition to relieving stress, self-hypnosis also moderates the activity of the immune system in response to stress. An increase in stress and fatigue occurs with a concomitant increase in the levels of T cells, B cells, and natural killer cells. Stress and anxiety are also associated with outbreaks of herpes virus. Self-hypnosis with dynamic imagery technique reduces depression and anxiety while decreasing the rates of infection and recurrence of herpes virus.

Hypnotic procedures for relieving anxiety are also useful for medical procedures and health conditions that are associated with anxiety. Migraines and chronic tension headaches are also associated with anxiety. Self-hypnosis training for individuals suffering from chronic tension headaches reduces the number and frequency of headaches as well as alleviates anxiety. Anticipated anxiety and pain related to childbirth among pregnant women, can also be countered which self-hypnosis training. Moreover, self-hypnosis training is also useful for the management of unexpected anxiety associated with cesarean section during childbirth. A clinically prominent medical condition associated with anxiety is irritable bowel syndrome (IBS). Individuals with classic IBS, atypical IBS, and IBS with significant psychopathology may benefit from self-hypnosis training. Hypnotic techniques including eye fixation, imagery, and progressive relaxation are useful for alleviating the symptoms of IBS. These symptoms include constipation, flatulence, abdominal pain, and bloating. Hypnotherapy also helps manage the symptoms of anxiety related to the onset of IBS. Improvement in the symptoms of IBS occurs due to hypnosis-mediated reduction in the psychological distress, somatization, and anxiety related to IBS.

Hypnotherapy in Anxiety Associated with Medical and Surgical Procedures

Hypnosis is also used with conventional and non-conventional medical procedures. Hypnosis reduces pain and anticipatory anxiety during acupuncture. Hypnosis with acupuncture is more efficacious than pure acupuncture. Self-hypnosis during radiological procedures is helpful for the relaxation of patients and reducing the occurrence of anticipatory pain and anxiety experiences. Individuals with self-hypnosis training are less likely to experience pain and require lesser medications as compared to individuals without self-hypnosis training during radiology procedures such as lumbar puncture and bone marrow aspiration. Individuals with high trait anxiety may require greater medications and have a prolonged treatment time, self-hypnosis training reduces the duration of treatment and reduces the need for medications in these individuals, regarding cancerous patients undergoing medical procedures. Hypnosis alleviates both procedure-related and anticipatory anxiety.

A significant proportion of patients undergoing surgery develop anxiety related to anesthesia and the fear of not waking up after the surgical procedure. Hypnotherapy conducted before the surgical interventions lead to lesser pain, state anxiety, and reduced duration of stay at the hospital. Relaxation and guided imagery during hypnotic procedures may lead to increased knee strength and reduced anxiety for reinjury of the joint, along with a reduction in pain in patients undergoing knee surgery. Adjunctive hypnotherapy with conscious sedation in plastic surgery is also useful for reducing anxiety, It reduces the need for drugs used for immobilizing the patients, anxiety, and postoperative vomiting and nausea. Individuals who received hypnotherapy reported greater surgical comfort and increase satisfaction with anesthesia in plastic surgeries. The use of imagery techniques in hypnotherapy for patients scheduled for elective surgical procedures is useful for lesser use of narcotic medications, reduced pain, and lesser anxiety before and after the operation. In coronary artery bypass patients, ego strengthening hypnotherapy reduces anxiety significantly, myocardial ischemia, and sympathetic activity of the heart while performing pericutaneous transluminal angioplasty. Self-hypnosis also counters dental anxiety and is used in oral surgical procedures. It reduces the requirement for intravenous sedation and also lowers the heart rate of the patient. As compared to patients who did not receive hypnotherapy, individuals who underwent hypnotherapy have more positive outcomes related to dental and oral surgical procedures. Hypnotherapy also reduces physiological parameters associated with oral surgical procedures. Hypnotherapy augments sedation in individuals with drug dependence.

Hypnotherapy in Medical Conditions Associated with Anxiety

Other groups of patients, who experience anxiety and pain, may also benefit from hypnotherapy and self-hypnosis training. Burn patients develop pain and anxiety, particularly associated with dressing changes. Similar to other stress-reducing strategies, self-hypnosis training is also useful for alleviating pain and anxiety associated with dressing changes in severely burned patients. The onset and increase in anxiety is a natural occurrence in patients who are diagnosed with cancer. A randomized study compared the outcomes of cancer-related anxiety in individuals who received hypnotherapy versus those who were subjected to breathing techniques for the alleviation of anxiety. Hypnotherapy improves the onset of acute anxiety attacks and causes cancer patients to experience less negative and more positive states of mood. Autogenic training, a form of self-hypnosis, reduces anxiety and arousal in cancer patients, improving their coping abilities in these individuals. Self-hypnosis also helps manage the perception of cancer patients about their environment being threatening and hostile. Self-hypnosis relieves the symptoms of cancer-related anxiety, as well as induces an overall sense of health and well-being. After receiving hypnotherapy and self-hypnosis training, cancer patients experience an increase in the motivation for fighting against cancer and also experience improved sleep, as compared to the sleeping patterns before receiving hypnotherapy or self-hypnosis training.

Conclusion

Self-hypnosis training and other forms of hypnotherapeutic procedures are useful measures for reducing anxiety and other anticipatory symptoms associated with medical procedures and diagnosis of several health conditions. burns patients, cancer patients, IBS patients, individuals suffering from chronic tension headaches, individuals scheduled for dental procedures, oral surgical interventions, colorectal surgeries, coronary artery bypass surgery, and radiological procedures benefit from self-hypnosis training, hypnotherapy relaxation, imagery, and deepening.

Chapter 14: Hypnosis for Smoking Cessation

Introduction

Tobacco smoking is a prevalent cause of preventable death across the globe. Tobacco smoking increases mortality associated with the onset of cancers and cardiovascular diseases. Tobacco smokers are subjected to premature death owing to tobacco smoking. Majority of the tobacco smokers are located in the low-income and middle-income regions of the world. Hypnotherapy is an effective clinical tool that is recognized and used by different medical professionals for the treatment and management of different health conditions. Hypnotherapy is also successful in alleviating the symptoms associated with IBS, chronic pain, cancer, and asthma. This chapter describes the use of hypnotherapy for smoking cessation.

Hypnotherapy for Cessation of Tobacco Smoking

There is an increase in the cessation rate in individuals who receive hypnotherapy, as compared to individuals who do not receive hypnotherapy or other forms of behavioral interventions for smoking cessation. Hypnotherapy is relatively more effective than nicotine replacement therapy in promoting smoking cessation and improving behavioral modification in tobacco smokers. Individuals receiving hypnotherapy with nicotine replacement therapy are more likely to become non-smokers after the set duration of therapy, as compared to individuals who receive nicotine replacement therapy only. The smoke-free state in individuals who receive hypnotherapy is attributed to mind-body interactions during hypnosis and the key suggestion phase of hypnotherapy. Hypnotherapy also increases motivation and self-confidence to diminish the desire to consume tobacco smoke. Hypnotherapy allows for the hypnotic practitioner to give effective suggestions for the cessation of tobacco smoking, as well as improves the responsiveness of the individuals to stop the consumption of tobacco smoke. Hypnotherapy is more efficacious than the relaxation session, in which no suggestions for cessation of tobacco smoking are provided by the therapist. Hypnotherapy can also be used with cognitive-behavioral therapy for the cessation of tobacco smoke and other health conditions such as IBS, cancer, and bronchial asthma. Moreover, individuals with a cardiac diagnosis are more likely to quit smoking as compared to individuals without a cardiac diagnosis or other underlying health conditions. (Barnes et al., 2019)

Hypnotherapy Sessions for Cessation of Tobacco Smoking

This session highlights the details of sessions of hypnotherapy for promoting the cessation of tobacco smoking.

In the first session of hypnotherapy for cessation of tobacco smoking, initial consultation with the patient is completed, and a rapport is established. The hypnotic practitioner acquires details about every aspect of the patient's life and about the underlying clinical problem of the patient. This session also includes a detailed discussion about the factors, which trigger the patient's desire to smoke, and may hinder the therapy process. These factors are also used as targets for hypnotherapy by the hypnotic practitioner. The hypnotic practitioner also investigates the relationship between cigarette smoking and stress. During the first session of hypnotherapy, the patient also communicates his or her expectations from the hypnotherapy sessions. The hypnotic practitioner also performs a behavioral assessment to learn about the behavior and cognition of the patient. The hypnotic techniques are also explained to the patient and all the queries are answered. Information acquired during this session of hypnotherapy is useful for suggestions and hypnotic techniques utilized in future sessions of hypnotherapy for a cessation of tobacco smoking.

During the second session of hypnotherapy for cessation of tobacco smoking, the action plan developed during the first session of hypnotherapy is reviewed as well as the smoking status and behavioral features of the patient are also discussed. After these steps, hypnosis is initiated, and suggestions are provided to the patients by the hypnotic practitioner. The hypnotic induction is performed, which is useful for increasing the concentration and focus of the subject while eliminating any distractions from the external environment. This facilitates the responsiveness of this subject towards suggestions made by the hypnotic practitioner in the later stages of hypnosis. During the stage of hypnosis, somnambulism is induced, the hypnotic state is further deepened, and the patient becomes more receptive to the suggestions during the hypnotherapy. The hypnotic practitioner then uses imagery associated with the problem, in this case, tobacco smoking. During hypnotherapy, the suggestions and positive imagery stimulate the client to develop a commitment to quitting tobacco smoking. The subject is also provided suggestions related to specific actions after awakening from the hypnotic state. During hypnotherapy, the subjects are also trained regarding self-hypnosis, which is also included in the homework assignment after the hypnotherapy session is over. Self-hypnosis inculcates the sense of greater control over the habits and facilitates the cessation of smoking.

During the third session of hypnotherapy, the patients are required to repeat self-hypnosis and offer suggestions for themselves. During this session, the action plan is reviewed, and the patients are assigned related homework and quick trance techniques with positive suggestions that are provided in the hypnotherapy session. During this session, the patients are also required to develop suggestions for the resolution of immediate problems, in this case, tobacco smoking.

The fourth and last session of hypnotherapy comprises a detailed discussion between the hypnotic practitioner and the therapy recipient about changes in behavior and the status of smoking. Activities of the prior week, related to smoking and associated behaviors, are also reviewed during the fourth session of hypnotherapy for cessation of tobacco smoking. During this session, the patients are hypnotized using deepening hypnotic techniques and imagery related to the problem. The practitioner also provides suggestions to facilitate the cessation of tobacco smoking. These may include direct suggestions and ego-strengthening suggestions. The patients and hypnotic practitioners also discuss the future treatment plans, as well as discuss the practice of self-hypnosis for increasing the cessation rate of tobacco smoking. During this session, the frequency of self-hypnosis and termination of hypnotherapy is also discussed with the patient. In the follow-up sessions, the hypnotic practitioner assesses the smoking behaviors of the patient and whether the patient is experiencing any cravings.

Conclusion

Tobacco smoking is a global problem which is associated with increased rates of death and the occurrence of health conditions including cardiovascular and pulmonary conditions. Different conventional and non-conventional therapeutic measures have been undertaken to facilitate the reduction and cessation of tobacco smoking. Hypnotherapy involves social interaction between the subject and hypnotic practitioner for the treatment and management of different health ailments. Hypnotherapy and self-hypnosis training are also useful techniques for facilitating the cessation of tobacco smoking, reducing craving, and improving the associated behaviors.

9. Appendix

In the following text passages, I will frequently switch back and forth between the formal and the informal speech. This is intentional. Depending on the personality of your client, one of these will be more suitable. It is up to your intuition which form you choose for which client within an exercise. There is no orthodox, right, or wrong way to do this.

Paced Breathing

You can do the following exercise with your clients at the beginning, middle, or end of the induction. Pacing promotes rapport between you and the client. It can be understood as a non-verbal trance induction. The suggestion text could be as follows:

And to help you access your subconscious mind, I now ask you to breathe deeply in and out five times.... "Breathe in......Very well, and out ...... Just so..... In.....and out again and keep going...v. Very good....You can now continue breathing normally..... That's it...j Just keep breathing.... calmly and deeply..... Just as your breathing is controlled all by itself by your subconscious mind."

In many cases, I hardly give any suggestions, but simply breathe noisily with the client.

Hypnosis in Exam Anxiety

Before we begin our session, please get seated in a comfortable position.

You can either lie or sit down. The important thing is that you feel comfortable and can relax a little. You do not have to do much. Just try to follow my voice and my words.

Do not force yourself to stay awake. Just let yourself go. Even if you digress for a moment or start dozing off, your subconscious can still absorb and process all the information.

Sometimes it can be quite pleasant to turn our attention inwards and encourage our body to relax. You can also do this by simply trying to imagine what I am asking you to do.

And as we know, we can imagine things much more vividly with our eyes closed. That is why I am asking you at this point to close your eyes for a moment. Just close your eyes and try to transform my words into inner images. So if I ask you right now to imagine the shape of your head, for example, and then I pause for a moment, then just create this image... you don't need to answer my question.

Can you imagine the distance between your earlobes? And the one between your eyes....now please become aware of the position of your tongue in your mouth...And how much distance is there is between your nose and the back of your head.....

Can you determine whether one arm is maybe heavier than the other?

......Can you feel how long your arms are from your shoulders to your fingertips?... Is there possibly a difference in temperature between one hand and the other? Or are both hands equally warm... or cold......?.

Imagine the width of your shoulders....Feel how much space there is between your shoulders.....Feel the pressure with which your back rests on the chair. Become aware of your whole upper body....Can you feel the weight you are resting on?...

Can you visualize your feet?...Where is each foot in relation to the other foot?...and what about the distance between your knees...Can you do a scan of your whole body? Starting with your head, you can become aware of the position of your arms, your hands, your torso, and your legs.

And just as you have succeeded in feeling and experiencing your outer body parts, you may now be able to feel and experience your inner body....

Now direct your attention even further inwards. By simply deepening this attention, you are beginning to relax a little more...I will now gently accompany you into this, for your most optimal state, in which your subconscious can become active for your goals today...

Your subconscious will accompany you into exactly the state, exactly the depth of trance, that it needs to transport the contents it wants to transport even better into your inner being and to let them work exactly there...

And while your subconscious mind is already starting to make the necessary arrangements by letting you calm down a bit...I will tell you a bit more about how hypnosis works in us...so that you can benefit from this session and its effect as much as possible....

Perhaps you can let go a little and free yourself from disturbing thought patterns by simply relying on your subconscious. Let your subconscious carry you...you don't have to do anything...because your subconscious helps you sink into the very trance that helps you integrate and process the goals of today's hypnosis....

You may perceive this state as a gentle relaxation, where you are carried as if on an ocean...an ocean of calm....

And if your subconscious wants to, it will carry you even deeper into this state...even deeper while your body can come to rest...deeper and deeper...while your psyche can now rest for the following moments....

And you don't have to do anything for it...You shouldn't do anything for it...You can't do anything for it...

It happens all by itself...trust your subconscious...

This state is as specific as can be. While one person will feel something slowly flowing inside them, for another it will feel like that moment on the border of the dream world...when we think more in images and inner processes feel more real to us than ever. A third person will just feel a gentle calmness slowly coming into him or her....

And exactly this state...whatever state your subconscious chooses for you, it is exactly the state it needs to let the contents of this session take effect in you....

So take this experience with an open mind and curiosity...free of any expectations of how this hypnosis should perhaps feel...rely on your subconscious and let go a little, and your subconscious will pave the way for you to achieve the goals of today's session....

Free yourself from pressure and follow my words...let them flow deep within you...while your subconscious mind will help itself to the content it needs to let the hypnosis work...gently....quietly...and sometimes quite subtly within you....

Your subconscious mind sets everything in motion that is relevant for today's topic....It knows how you feel about hypnosis...it knows all the blockades and old burdens that contribute to the perpetuation of your problem....

And likewise it knows all your desires and goals [(insert session content here]) ", to be free of fear....free of that limiting feeling...free from that feeling of standing like a deer in the headlights of a car...experience exam situations with the calm and gentle serenity that lies deep within each of us...."

And while your subconscious mind starts to work through these areas inside you...you can support it by taking three deep breaths in and exhaling for a long time, you can then continue to breathe normally. Very gently and calmly.....just as your breathing is controlled by your inner self....

[At this point breathe in and out together with the client, or accompany the breathing with short, simple sentences.].

You can now just let your breath flow gently again. Meanwhile, your subconscious has already initiated everything to work through the unhealthy thought and behavior patterns that have prevented you from [(insert session content here]) taking the exam in a light-hearted way with just the right amount of positive stress to be able to concentrate and pass the tests without any problems...

Your subconscious accompanies you from the beginning to the end of your life...it is present at every moment and knows every second, every experience and every feeling that have made you the person you are today....

Like an iceberg, the core, and foundation of your personality is hidden beneath the visible surface. And that is our subconscious...the gigantic sum of all the insights in your life. And this is accurately where hypnosis comes in...

Maybe now you can better understand why you can just let yourself go;, give the control and responsibility for your fear to your subconscious.

And you can help your subconscious to work for you by briefly thinking about what you actually want to achieve with today's session...

Imagine it... spontaneously... just as it comes to your mind.....

Imagine that you are already there...the hypnosis has done its work in cooperation with your subconscious and you are now exactly where you want to be...You are now feeling exactly what you want to feel….and while you are doing this, bringing this to your inner mind…your subconscious is already working on the very places, the areas and blockages that may have been responsible for perpetuating the problems up to now…

Take a moment for this again…and visualize it…

[Pause a moment here]

Very good!

Everything is now perfectly prepared within you… Your subconscious can transport the following contents deep into your inner being in order to let them work there…

Main practice [The following contents can be repeated several times depending on how fast you speak of speech and the remaining time.].

It will work causative around deeply existing roots and triggers of your exam anxiety to eliminate them. And at the same time it will work on the symptoms of this fear in the here and now and dissolve them bit by bit…and this irrational fear will become a meaningless issue…an issue that has completely lost its emotional relevance….

The words I have used are conscientiously chosen and many others have been able to gain therapeutic value from their meaning….

So just let the words work on you…They are like a canvas on which the subconscious can become active to give you the space your psyche needs to allow you to take your exams in the best possible way….

Just accompany my words for this with your thoughts...then your subconscious will pick out the contents and information that are important for your emotional growth and everything that has to do with the taking of future exams....

Now your subconscious checks everything inside you and optimizes all processes that make a smooth exam procedure possible for you...

Did you know that exam anxiety is a widespread phenomenon? This is nothing unusual... such fears are among the most frequent causes for the use of hypnosis...

In fact, such feelings are among the best researched and studied areas of application in hypnotherapy....

Whereby the reasons can be quite different...while one person doesn't like the pressure of being on call to access their knowledge...another may simply not like being tested, while in a private setting the exercises and tasks seem completely effortless to them... some also simply worry unnecessarily about the assessment...the consequences of the exam... the things that might happen if they don't pass... what questions might be asked. Yes, some get uncomfortable just thinking about an exam....

And all this is not unusual at all...it is a natural and human reaction that we have known for a long time... these reactions and sensations are protective mechanisms...like a security system triggered by our deepest instincts... maintained and reinforced by the experiences we make....

And these processes in many cases only need a little fine tuning... to meet the demands of everyday life...to work through those exaggerated and unnecessary reactions such as nervousness or fear... to become factually and emotionally irrelevant....

And today we are working exactly on this goal...so that you can master exams with confidence...

For this I would like you to picture exactly that...imagine that an exam is a completely normal and emotionally unremarkable situation for you....

Imagine that exams are such an everyday occurrence for you that you yourself would want to take the exam, and that you would not feel anything unpleasant about it ...

Even though this may sound unusual at first, I want you to imagine exactly that...imagine yourself as this experienced person for whom exams are something completely normal and worry-free...

Picture it in your mind's eye...you... taking an exam smoothly and free from nervousness...Yyou know you have all the skills you need for it...Yyou know you have done enough to prepare for the exam in the best possible way...and that either way your life will go on after the exam...Tthe exam is just another stage in your life that will open more doors regardless of the outcome...Yyou will take exams the way you want to and intend to !

You are completely confident and self-assured in exam situations...like a lawyer who has taken many exams and examinations and for whom it is part of everyday life to recall his knowledge every few months...exams can be a relaxing and beneficial experience once they have been taken...for this your subconscious can simply become active....

And as you are creating all these images, your subconscious mind can learn from all these inner images and concepts to free you from these fears and discomforts that were previously associated with exams. It will search within you for all the possibilities, experiences, and stimuli to help you deal with exams in a healthy way. If it finds something there that is responsible for perpetuating the problem, then it will readjust and reassess that until it has let the last bit of insecurity flow from you...so that you can face future exam situations without concern...free from fear...free from discomfort...you are completely free.....

And a thought that used to stress you out can gradually become less and less important...a normal and everyday occurrence that leaves you completely calm and completely relaxed...

Your subconscious mind builds a new foundation upon which a healthy and free person can mature...by resolving the issues from the core of your problem and allowing you...to walk into future situations strong and confident....You are serene and free...you are in control and relaxed when it matters. Exams are something completely normal for you. Situations that may have made you uncomfortable before, you can now look at, free of emotion. You are strong and consolidated in your abilities and knowledge...you know what you can do and your subconscious is now your friend...it will help you to become exactly that and to master future challenges....in complete peace...the following nights and days your subconscious will continue to work on that and with every waking up it will strengthen these newly gained abilities... step by step...

until it has brought this experience completely in line with your person...in complete peace...the following nights and days your subconscious will continue to work and with every waking up it will strengthen these newly gained abilities step by step until it has brought this experience completely in line with your person...

[repeat the last paragraph]

...that's it...

I know that your subconscious has already been able to do a lot for you. It has been able to change one or two things...nuances inside you to help you. Your subconscious will be your best friend in the future...it will make you strong where you need strength...it will give you safety in the moments you need to feel safe...and it will let you benefit from all its abilities....as it has let others benefit too.... who listened to a simple hypnosis and absorbed the words deeply and focused their attention on inner processes....to then realize how much better they feel...how much easier and less stressful dealing with exams suddenly becomes... over and over again I experience exactly that...how a client can't really feel that feeling of unease anymore....

I am always amazed how former clients suddenly mention exams in such a light-hearted way and how they were able to develop new healthy thinking and behavior patterns...

And your subconscious has made all this possible for you by triggering the following suggestions within you once again...

What else should it let flow away from you in the following nights that has been possibly blocking or weighing on you so far...?

What attitudes and emotions can it optimize to enable you to deal with exam situations even better ?

For this purpose, the subconscious regulates everything inside you in order to change everything that it can already accomplish for you today...

In addition to our experiences and knowledge, that are partly responsible for our perception, it is especially our autonomic nervous system that is responsible for negative reactions in stressful situations...

It regulates your blood pressure, your pulse, the opening of your sweat glands as well as your heartbeat...and in a really dangerous situation, this can be helpful...but for taking exams, it is set too sensitive in some people...And the sum of the sensations that you then get, we generally call stress...And this stress can be regulated by the subconscious mind simply by regulating the level of the tension you feel... letting you shut down in important situations and relieving the stress....

This process will help you to better deal with this stress, which is not actually anything unhealthy, but just a reaction of your nervous system...by checking everything inside you and re-evaluating everything that has to do with stress... and integrating and adjusting it in a healthy way....

You will notice how this process will slowly take shape....

Your consciousness is now emptied and your subconscious has cleared itself of anything that is stressing you or blocking you from an ordinary exam experience. You will feel relief spreading within you. In the coming nights and days, your subconscious will reorganize your inner self and noticeably fill up the newly acquired free space with additional energy.

You will also feel how much strength the letting go will give you, h. How much inner harmony and well-being you feel and how good it feels to have been freed from all the ballast. You will already feel the positive change inside you.

Perhaps you will realize how something is changing in a positive way within you or around you. Perhaps you will realize how much easier it is for you to achieve your goals. Maybe aone or the other problem in your life will be solved... where you might not have expected a solution at all.

Your subconscious is now free. It now has even more power to support you in everything that is good for you. This process of letting go has already freed many people and I can imagine that you and your environment can also benefit from it positively.

Hypnosis Intervention to Release Blockages

The following hypnosis program helps you to work through existing blockages and burdens from your past. These blockages represent all inhibiting or straining burdens from the past. As a result of trauma, hurtful events, and painful memories, a burden often builds up inside us, which we then carry with us in our daily lives and which can be partly responsible for maintaining unhealthy ways of thinking and behaving. All of us are familiar with the feeling of somehow not being able to move on, and of simply not being able to come to terms with some experiences.

With this exercise, you will be able to emotionally realign yourself with the problem areas that are still blocking you. To enjoy the following session as much as possible and to benefit from its effect, I would like to ask you to think again about the things of which you would like to let go off. Think about them again and try to accept the following contents with an open mind and with curiosity.

Before we begin our session, take a comfortable position. You can lie down or sit for this purpose. The main thing is that you feel comfortable and can relax. You do not have to do much. Just try to follow my voice and my words. Do not force yourself to stay awake. Just let yourself go. Even if you digress for a moment or start dozing off, your subconscious can still absorb and process all the information. Occasionally it can be quite pleasant to turn your attention inwards and encourage your body to relax. You can do this easily, by trying to simply turn what I will ask you into inner images and just visualizing this.

And as we know, we can imagine things much more vividly with our eyes closed. That is why I ask you at this point to close your eyes for a moment. Just close your eyes and transform my words into inner images... So when I will ask you in a moment if you can picture the shape of your head, for example, and I then pause for a moment, just picture it...You don't have to answer my question.

Can you imagine the distance between your earlobes and that between your eyes...now please become aware of the position of your tongue in your mouth...And how much distance is there between your nose and the back of your head...

Can you tell if one arm is perhaps heavier than the other? ...Can you feel how long your arms are from your shoulders to your fingertips?...Is there possibly a difference in temperature between one hand and the other? Or are both hands equally warm or cold.......?.

Imagine the width of your shoulders....Feel how much space there is between your shoulders.....Feel the pressure with which your back rests on the chair back. Become aware of your whole upper body....can you feel the weight you are resting on?...?

Can you feel your feet? ...what distance is there between one foot and the other foot?...and what is the distance between your knees......?

Can you do a whole body scan this way ? Starting with your head, ...become aware of the position of your arms, your hands, your torso, and your legs. And just as you have succeeded in feeling and experiencing your body in this way.... you can turn your attention even further inwards...

Once you achieve this experience.....the experience of being held without limits, carried as if in an ocean of peace and safety, bit by bit you can feel a deep calm and trust throughout your whole body....

Your subconscious will now guide you into exactly the trance that fits what we want to achieve today.... Your subconscious mind will build connections to all the areas inside you that are significant so that you can achieve what we have set out to do today.

Because your subconscious mind knows exactly what we want to achieve here and now... It knows how you feel about hypnosis and it knows your wishes and above all, it knows your expectations. And now it will begin to accompany you step by step into exactly the right state in which it can optimally work for your goals today. To support your subconscious in this process, please breathe in and out ...deeply ...and calmly three times.

[(Include breath pacing here])

You can now continue to breathe normally, you do not need to worry about your breathing any further.

Your subconscious mind now gently controls the breathing in just the right way so that it can accompany your autonomic nervous system into a pleasant state. So just let your breath flow gently and let the subconscious mind take control... And by now the subconscious mind inside you has already become active and it will start to achieve your goals and prepare everything for the hypnosis to work ...the hypnosis can work in an optimal way inside you...

Our subconscious mind is able to influence the temperature of our hands, the width, or narrowness of our blood vessels, the tension of our striated muscles and many other unconscious processes...You can support your subconscious mind in getting into the state it needs by focusing your thoughts on what you actually want to achieve with hypnosis....

Imagine what you want to achieve with this hypnosis session...

Imagine it spontaneously... Just as it comes to your mind.

Think about what would be different if you achieved the goal of this hypnosis. Visualize what would be different then or what would be better... Let me give you a moment to go through these goals and expectations again mentally...And by re-living your goals in your mind, your subconscious will initiate step by step all the necessary processes to bring about the desired change. I will give you a brief moment so that you can imagine this again...

Good....

Meanwhile your subconscious has prepared everything for you.

And it will carry you deeper and deeper and step by step into this pleasant state....

Deeper and deeper and gently...more and more...

Just follow the words and let them flow deeply into you....

Inside you, your subconscious mind sets everything up all by itself so that the hypnosis can work within you. And if your thoughts wander for a moment, then simply return to my words. You will not miss or forget anything. Your subconscious integrates and processes all information, even without your intervention. It hears everything and understands everything. It now carries you further and further into this gentle trance, step by step...deeper and deeper...and all by itself....exactly like this, deeper and deeper. Today your subconscious will have the opportunity to simply let go.

During this session it will free you in an intensive way from all the old burdens that are hindering in the present and that you can now releaselet go off...

To make space for new positive experiences...

To make space for your personal goals...

And to give you the opportunity to finally get where you want to go....

You can adopt the following section one-to-one or adapt it specifically for your patients by replacing the key points by the client's specific problem area or an explicit problem.

Your subconscious will surely find something that it simply wants to get rid of here and now...

In the course of time, every person has something that accumulates...

Unhealthy basic assumptions...

Fears... Emotional blocks...t Tensions...i Injuries...

For each of us it can be a beneficial experience to simply let go of this ballast that is no longer needed... To let what holds us back and burdens us, simply flow away from us...

And our subconscious can help us to do just that, by sorting out everything inside us and simply letting go of what we perhaps no longer need, what stands in our way more than being of any use....

We sometimes know exactly what is flowing out, which issues are still weighing heavily on our hearts, but in some cases it is simply little things that at first don't seem so burdensome to us, which, we think, would not play such a big role for the subconscious mind....

But our subconscious knows exactly what is a burden for us, it classifies everything exactly and it can sort everything in such a way that it can let go of these old burdens, here and now....

Everything that your subconscious wants to free you from today, it will now let flow into your hands and it will first collect it there.... And during this session, when it has been able to work through whateverything that is important to the here and now... then it will let what has been collected in your hands flow from you and free you from it....

It will now begin to release all old burdens.... All blockages... And let all unhealthy thought patterns flow away....

All the thought processes from which it wants to free you today, it will let flow from your upper body over to your upper and lower arms and into your hands, collecting them in there...

Perhaps you can start to notice how what is flowing from your inner being, deep from your subconscious, is now flowing through your arms into your hands....You may slowly notice how all this ballast begins to fill your hands until they are full and heavy....Your subconscious cleanses your entire inner being and pays attention to every little thing... It has been with you all your life and therefore knows every single second, every emotion, every injury, every little nuance in your body...

It can understand and interpret the connections within you.... trust your subconscious.... it will only let flow into your hands what it thinks you can let go of....

In doing so, it frees you from everything that has inhibited you up to now and was responsible for the perpetuation of your problems...

on the physiological... psychological... mental... and emotional levels...

It has access to all areas of your person and everything it wants to let flow, everything it wants to let go of, it now lets flow into your hands....

Maybe you can feel that something is loosening up somewhere inside you, maybe you can feel it getting a little warm or tingling somewhere, or that something that was tense before is now relaxing and all this is at this moment flowing into your hands... Feel how it simply lets go of the ballast that has accumulated over the years....

Feel how it dissolves all the obstacles within you and lets them flow into your hands....

From your memories...

Deep from your soul...

Deep from your heart...

Yes, deep from within you and your subconscious....

Wherever your subconscious wants to let go of something, it will do so now., Iit will let it flow from you....

In our subconscious, there are always things that we don't need anymore and that we should perhaps let go of... In every person there is an emotional ballast that accumulates. Sometimes it is ballast that you would not even think is important for you... Sometimes it is things that you had actually thought you had long since finished with... Sometimes it is things that you are not even aware of... But of course there are also things that you know are a problem for you and hinder you, things that you would also like to process yourself.... That's how it is with every human being... And now you can let go...

Feel inside yourself and observe what is happening in you right now, what images may appear to you and what thoughts may arise in you, yes, what the words bring about in you....

Now your subconscious has the opportunity to finish with everything that it might have wanted to let go of for a long time, it can now let everything flow from you that has been weighing you down so far....

Feel into yourself and feel how your subconscious sorts out your inner self one step at a time... How it lets go of all the things it has perhaps long wanted to get rid of...

It is not repressed, no, you can really finally let it go and it can no longer be a burden to you, no longer cause you pain, no longer block you....

These fears, these memories of situations and people, yes, of things that hurt you in your childhood, your youth, and the present, your subconscious now releases all of this into your hands....

Often things come into flow that you would not have expected, these little things that you are not aware of at first, but which can be an enormous ballast for the subconscious and all this comes into flow at such a moment.... And the more it flows, the more relief and well-being you will feel inside...

Just take a look inside yourself and see if you can notice what is flowing from you, if you recognize something or maybe not, because your subconscious mind uses this opportunity to allow everything to flow from you that has been a burden to you until now....

And the more that flows from you.... the more your subconscious lets go, the more relieved you feel.

I am about to give your subconscious the opportunity to continue its work and to let everything flow from you that it wants to get rid of... and when it has released everything, then it will let go of what has been collected in your hands, it will let it flow from you.... And you will be able to say goodbye to all the things that have been weighing you down....

And when your subconscious frees you from more and more ballast, I would like to take you on a little journey and talk to you about the topic...

[At this point, if necessary, the main application can follow. If only a blockage and legacy dissolution is desired, the hypnosis session ends with the next paragraph.]

And meanwhile your subconscious has released everything that it wanted to let go of, it could free you from everything that was weighing on you and your hands are empty again.....

And your subconscious gets the opportunity to let go right now....

It can free you today in an intense but smooth way from all the ballast it wants to get rid of.... to make space for new positive experiences... to make space for your goals and to give you the freedom to achieve what is important for you... here and now... .....

Over time, our subconscious mind accumulates a lot. Like an iceberg, it remains hidden deep beneath the surface and grows there with each experience.

Over time, plenty of things accumulate inside...

These can be small annoyances and fears, worries, physical blockages, emotions or stress...

And every so often it can be incredibly comforting to simply let go of what we no longer need, of what is more of a burden than a benefit.

Your subconscious can process everything and free you from all unnecessary ballast that is currently holding you back or standing in your way. It can free you from all of that.

Our subconscious mind sometimes moves quite big issues to do this, but sometimes also small things whose influences we are not really aware of.

The subconscious can classify these experiences all by itself and weigh up for itself what it wants to let go of, here and now.

And it will immediately let everything it wants to release flow into your hands and first collect it there. And later it will let go of everything it has collected when it has finished its cleansing.

Perhaps you feel something slowly beginning to flow....a gentle feeling running along your arm....

You might also feel your hands filling up more and more... and how they become heavier and fuller.....as more and more flows into them...

And your subconscious frees you from everything, it cleanses your inner being, and it can watch every detail of your life again like a film, it knows every moment, every memory, every thought, and every single cell in your body.

Connections that may not be clear to you rationally can be understood by your subconscious. You can trust it. It will only let flow from you what should really be let go of today. However, it makes sure that it does not forget anything that might be important.

It frees you from all blockages and everything that has burdened you....on the emotional...cognitive...and physical levels.

It has access to all levels of your personality, and it releases everything it no longer needs into your hands.

You can feel it releasing this ballast that has accumulated over time and dissolving the blockades inside you...from your feelings...from your memories...from your body...deep from your subconscious and deep from your inner being...

No matter where inside you, something needs to be released... your subconscious can let it go now...

Maybe you can feel something starting to release in your body. Maybe you can feel something in your body getting warm or tingling... something that was stiff and tense before can now be light and relaxed... and all of this flows into your hands...

Our subconscious takes in all our experiences, so there is always something it wants to let go of. Over time, everyone accumulates something that wants to be released go of.

Sometimes it's the things that weigh us down that we otherwise don't pay much attention to....Such as things that have touched us......things that we thought we had long since finished with.......things that we perhaps don't even think about any more...but sometimes also things that we are perfectly clear about...that we know should be free go of....

It's like that for many people...

And today... here and now... is the time to let go....

Just look inside yourself and see what is going on inside you right now...observe what thoughts arise for you....

What memories arise, yes, observe what images appear in front of your inner eye.

Feel what the words are doing to you. Feel how your subconscious gradually cleans up inside you. And how it lets go of everything it has wanted to bring to an end for a long time... You don't need to be afraid of forgetting something... you will finally be able to put it behind you. It can no longer stand in your way or be a burden to you...burdening, stressful feelings and memories of people or situations...experiences that may have affected you over the years...from your childhood, youth or in the present...let them flow into your hands. Now your subconscious has the opportunity to let go off everything that it may have wanted to let go of for a long time. Now it can come to terms with what it may have wanted to come to terms with for a long time. Your subconscious lets all this flow into your open hands. Look inside yourself and see if you can perceive what is flowing. Whether you can recognize something or not... your subconscious is using the opportunity to throw off a ballast. Occasionally it's just little things that the conscious mind doesn't actively deal with. Things that you would never have thought could be a burden to the subconscious. Nevertheless, they are coming into flow right now.

The more ballast that is collected in your hands, the more relief you feel rising in you at the same time. The more unusable energy your subconscious has released, the more relief you feel. I will now remain silent until your subconscious has finished its job. When everything has been released that it wants to let go of, then it will begin to let everything flow out of your hands and throw everything away. It will let it flow away. You can meanwhile say goodbye to the things that have been burdening your inner being unnoticed. The more that flows away, the greater and stronger will be the feeling of relief within you. I will now remain silent as long as your subconscious is at work...

Until it has completely emptied your hands.

[Now 10 seconds of silence.]

Feel how relief expands inside of you. Further and further and further. Feel your relief getting stronger inside you. Stronger and stronger and stronger. It flows more and more...and more and more from you. More and more and more. More and more. And on and on. Your hands are now empty and your subconscious has freed itself from everything that has burdened or blocked you. You will feel relief spreading inside you. In the coming nights and days, your subconscious will reorganize your inner self and perceptibly fill up the newly acquired space inside you with additional energy. You will also feel how much strength releasing these blockages will give you.... How much inner harmony and well-being you feel and how good it feels to have been freed from all the ballast. You will already feel the positive change inside you. You may realize how something in you or around you is changing for the better. Perhaps you will realize how much easier it will be for you to achieve your goals. Maybe one or the other problem in your life will be resolved... where you might not have expected a solution to be found at all. Your subconscious is now free. It now has even more power to support you in everything that is good for you.

The release process has already set many people free and I can imagine that you and your environment will also gain from it positively.

References

Williamson, A. (2019). What is hypnosis, and how might it work?
Palliative Care: Research and Treatment, 12, 117822421982658.
https://doi.org/10.1177/1178224219826581

Valentine, K. E., Milling, L. S., Clark, L. J., & Moriarty, C. L.
(2019). The Efficacy of Hypnosis as a Treatment for Anxiety: A
Meta-Analysis. International Journal of Clinical and Experimental
Hypnosis, 67(3), 336–363. https://doi.org/10.1080/
00207144.2019.1613863

Jensen, M. P., Adachi, T., Tomé-Pires, C., Lee, J., Osman, Z. J.,
& Miró, J. (2014). Mechanisms of Hypnosis:Toward the
Development of a Biopsychosocial Model. International Journal
of Clinical and Experimental Hypnosis, 63(1), 34–75.
https://doi.org/10.1080/00207144.2014.961875

Hammond, D. C. (2013). A Review of the History of Hypnosis
Through the Late 19th Century. American Journal of Clinical
Hypnosis, 56(2), 174–191. https://doi.org/10.1080/
00029157.2013.826172

Medknow Publications. (2011, May). Table 1 : Correct responses
on hypnotherapy Statement Correct response,... ResearchGate;
ResearchGate. https://www.researchgate.net/figure/Correct-
responses-on-hypnotherapy-Statement-Correct-response-N-You-
do-not-remain_tbl4_51696908

Coulton, D. (1966). Writing Techniques in Hypnotherapy.
American Journal of Clinical Hypnosis, 8(4), 287–298.
https://doi.org/10.1080/00029157.1966.10402508

Ruzyla-Smith, P., Barabasz, A., Barabasz, M., & Warner, D. (1995). Effects of Hypnosis on the Immune Response: B-Cells, T-Cells, Helper and Suppressor Cells. American Journal of Clinical Hypnosis, 38(2), 71–79. https://doi.org/10.1080/00029157.1995.10403185

Hasan, S. S., Whorwell, P. J., Miller, V., Morris, J., & Vasant, D. H. (2021). Six vs 12 Sessions of Gut-focused Hypnotherapy for Irritable Bowel Syndrome: A Randomized Trial. Gastroenterology, 160(7), 2605-2607.e3. https://doi.org/10.1053/j.gastro.2021.02.058

Barnes, J., McRobbie, H., Dong, C. Y., Walker, N., & Hartmann-Boyce, J. (2019). Hypnotherapy for smoking cessation. Cochrane Database of Systematic Reviews, 2019(6). https://doi.org/10.1002/14651858.cd001008.pub3

hypnotherapy for aniety - Google Search. (2020). Google.com. https://www.google.com/search?q=hypnotherapy+for+aniety&oq=hypnotherapy+for+aniety&

About the Author

Jean-Maurice Cecilia-Menzel is an alternative practitioner of psychotherapy and a trained neurofeedback therapist. A three-year degree in health and social care, two years of training in psychotherapeutic work and ongoing research round off his career to date. He practices as an alternative practitioner of psychotherapy in his own office in Munich.

Read more at https://www.neurofeedback-praxis-muenchen.de.